# Contents

LETTER FROM PERF EXECUTIVE DIRECTOR . . . . . . . . . . . . . . . . . . . . . . . . . . . . . . . . . . . . . . . . . . . . . . II
LETTER FROM TARGET . . . . . . . . . . . . . . . . . . . . . . . . . . . . . . . . . . . . . . . . . . . . . . . . . . . . . . . . . . . . III
LETTER FROM THE DIRECTOR OF THE COPS OFFICE. . . . . . . . . . . . . . . . . . . . . . . . . . . . . . . . . . . . . IV
ACKNOWLEDGMENTS . . . . . . . . . . . . . . . . . . . . . . . . . . . . . . . . . . . . . . . . . . . . . . . . . . . . . . . . . . . . . V
INTRODUCTION . . . . . . . . . . . . . . . . . . . . . . . . . . . . . . . . . . . . . . . . . . . . . . . . . . . . . . . . . . . . . . . . . . 1
  Promising Crime Fighting Strategies. . . . . . . . . . . . . . . . . . . . . . . . . . . . . . . . . . . . . . . . . . . . . . . . . 1
  Results Show that More Agencies Plan To Adopt Predictive Policing and Intelligence-Led Policing . . . . . . . . . . 2
  Considerations for Appropriate Use of Predictive Policing Strategies. . . . . . . . . . . . . . . . . . . . . . . . . . . . . . . 7
TAILORING PARTNERSHIPS TO MAXIMIZE PUBLIC SAFETY. . . . . . . . . . . . . . . . . . . . . . . . . . . . . . . . 10
  Police Foundations: A Promising Partnership to Help Bridge Funding Gaps . . . . . . . . . . . . . . . . . . . . . 11
  Building Partnerships with Federal Law Enforcement Agencies . . . . . . . . . . . . . . . . . . . . . . . . . . . . . 12
  Partnerships with Universities and Other Researchers: Potential Growth Area for the Future . . . . . . . . . . . . . . 13
  Albuquerque Police Partner with Business Groups and Sandia National Laboratories. . . . . . . . . . . . . . . . . . . 15
  A Partnership between Police and Pawn Shops to Reduce Theft . . . . . . . . . . . . . . . . . . . . . . . . . . . . 19
IMPLEMENTING STRATEGIES TO INCREASE EFFICIENCY . . . . . . . . . . . . . . . . . . . . . . . . . . . . . . . . . 21
  Reducing Police Response to Minor Crimes. . . . . . . . . . . . . . . . . . . . . . . . . . . . . . . . . . . . . . . . . . . 21
  Additional Cost Saving Strategies for Consideration . . . . . . . . . . . . . . . . . . . . . . . . . . . . . . . . . . . . 24
  Private Security and Off-Duty Employment: Opportunities and Challenges . . . . . . . . . . . . . . . . . . . . . 25
FUTURE TRENDS IN TECHNOLOGY . . . . . . . . . . . . . . . . . . . . . . . . . . . . . . . . . . . . . . . . . . . . . . . . . . 27
  Police Increasingly Are Using Social Media. . . . . . . . . . . . . . . . . . . . . . . . . . . . . . . . . . . . . . . . . . . 27
  The Nationwide Public Safety Broadband Network Will Have a Major Impact on Policing . . . . . . . . . . . . . . . 29
  Next Generation 911: Benefits and Challenges . . . . . . . . . . . . . . . . . . . . . . . . . . . . . . . . . . . . . . . . 30
  Real Time Crime Centers Are Contributing to Crime Fighting. . . . . . . . . . . . . . . . . . . . . . . . . . . . . . 33
  Cybercrime Represents a Major Emerging Issue for Law Enforcement . . . . . . . . . . . . . . . . . . . . . . . . 33
  Exploring GPS Applications . . . . . . . . . . . . . . . . . . . . . . . . . . . . . . . . . . . . . . . . . . . . . . . . . . . . . 35
  Using Technology to Help Fill Personnel Gaps . . . . . . . . . . . . . . . . . . . . . . . . . . . . . . . . . . . . . . . . 36
THE ORGANIZATIONAL STRUCTURE OF POLICING,
AND THE NEXT GENERATION OF LAW ENFORCEMENT . . . . . . . . . . . . . . . . . . . . . . . . . . . . . . . . . . 38
  Does the Current Environment Require New Types of Leadership? . . . . . . . . . . . . . . . . . . . . . . . . . . 38
  Thinking Big to Reduce Crime and Address Gaps in Community Relationships. . . . . . . . . . . . . . . . . . 39
  Considerations for a New Organizational Structure . . . . . . . . . . . . . . . . . . . . . . . . . . . . . . . . . . . . . 40
  New Roles for Retired Officers . . . . . . . . . . . . . . . . . . . . . . . . . . . . . . . . . . . . . . . . . . . . . . . . . . . 41
CONCLUSION: SOME OF THE DETAILS ARE UNCLEAR,
BUT THE FUTURE OF POLICING LOOKS GOOD . . . . . . . . . . . . . . . . . . . . . . . . . . . . . . . . . . . . . . . . . 42
APPENDIXES . . . . . . . . . . . . . . . . . . . . . . . . . . . . . . . . . . . . . . . . . . . . . . . . . . . . . . . . . . . . . . . . . . . 46
APPENDIX A: Definitions of Policing Strategies. . . . . . . . . . . . . . . . . . . . . . . . . . . . . . . . . . . . . . . . . . 46
APPENDIX B: PERF Survey Results . . . . . . . . . . . . . . . . . . . . . . . . . . . . . . . . . . . . . . . . . . . . . . . . . . 47
APPENDIX C: "Future of Policing" Executive Session Attendees . . . . . . . . . . . . . . . . . . . . . . . . . . . . . . 64

# Letter from PERF Executive Director

This report details the findings from a project in which the Police Executive Research Forum (PERF), with support from the COPS Office and from Target, worked with police chiefs and other experts to consider a broad and important topic: future trends in policing.

There are a lot of fundamental changes happening in policing. Every day we read about new technologies being used by police departments, ranging from "body cameras" worn by officers and automated license plate readers to analytical software designed to predict when and where crimes are likely to occur in a city. Cybercrime is a major development that local police departments are starting to explore. Demographic changes are affecting the types of people who enter the policing profession. The economic crisis that began in 2008 was a wake-up call that police budgets are not sacrosanct; today's police agencies to some extent are competing with private security agencies. Today's communities demand more accountability and transparency from their police. And police departments are finding new ways to use social media and other strategies for communicating with their communities.

All of these factors add up to a feeling that policing in the 21st century changes more in a year than it changed in a decade a generation ago. And these changes are not just about finding new ways to reduce crime; they go deeper, to evaluating the basic mission of the police, and what people want from the police.

The purpose of this "Future Trends in Policing" project was to ask police leaders to take a step back from their daily operations and everyday crises, and consider the emerging issues that are changing policing in the most fundamental ways. We conducted a survey of police departments, and you will see the results of that survey mentioned throughout this report. And we held a one-day Summit at Target headquarters in Minneapolis, at which experienced police executives and up-and-coming leaders described the changes that are happening in their departments, and where they see these changes taking us in the future.

This project would not have been possible without funding from the Office of Community Oriented Policing Services, with additional support from the Target Corporation. PERF is grateful for this support.

Chuck Wexler, Executive Director
Police Executive Research Forum

# Letter from Target

Dear colleagues,

Target's priority is creating a safe and secure environment—for our guests, our team members, and the communities where we do business. When it comes to protecting our physical stores, digital data, and surrounding neighborhoods, we know that one of the best investments we can make is partnering with law enforcement and public-safety agencies. For more than two decades, our Target & BLUE initiative has built and maintained public-private partnerships at national, state, and local levels to defend against any threat to that safety and security.

*Future Trends in Policing* is an example of such collaboration between public and private sectors. Thanks to the leadership of the U.S. Department of Justice's COPS Office, both groups came together to discuss and develop solutions for society's public-safety challenges.

This publication reflects those interactions, including the outcomes of a national forum and survey we hosted with the COPS Office and PERF to examine the changing practices of policing. Those findings—which range from the most pressing issues today to how new technology is used—shed light on shifting trends in policing, give insight into the future of law enforcement, and help inform new approaches for solving emerging issues.

At Target, we honor the work of law enforcement, realizing its critical role in the orderly operation of commerce and communities, and offer our continued appreciation and gratitude to all who put their lives on the line every day. We're grateful for the opportunity to share our resources and expertise to help build safer and stronger communities where individuals, families, and businesses flourish, and I look forward to continuing our work together.

Regards,

Ralph Boelter, Vice President
Corporate Security, Target Corporation

# Letter from the Director of the COPS Office

Dear colleagues,

In partnership with the Police Executive Research Forum (PERF) and Target, I am pleased to present *Future Trends in Policing*—featuring the results of a national forum and survey that examined the changing practices of policing. Specifically, the focus was on new technologies and strategies such as: predictive policing; the importance of building strong partnerships with the community, academia, and federal law enforcement agencies; the use of social media to disseminate information as well as gather intelligence; the growing threat of cybercrime; and changes in workforce demographics that may result in new organizational structures for police agencies. The forum and survey helped frame the thoughts and practices of police, researchers, private sector partners, and other experts.

This publication embodies the knowledge and consensus of the key stakeholders who were present at the forum, participated in the survey, and represented the public's best interest in regards to public safety. The COPS Office, PERF, and Target facilitated an honest discussion between experts of key fields by acting as an independent arbiter on the issue of the future of public safety.

By developing effective strategies in public safety and communicating these strategies to all officers *and* the public, law enforcement will gain the advantage of strong relationships with internal, external, and political audiences. I hope you will find this publication helpful in your local efforts, and we encourage you to share this publication, as well as your success, with other law enforcement practitioners.

Sincerely,

Ronald L. Davis, Director
Office of Community Oriented Policing Services

# Acknowledgments

PERF would like to thank the U.S. Justice Department's Office of Community Oriented Policing Services (COPS Office) and Target Corporation for supporting this examination of emerging issues that local law enforcement agencies are confronting and that will have an impact on policing in the next two to five years. We are grateful to the COPS Office Director Ronald Davis and former Acting Director Joshua Ederheimer for recognizing the importance of identifying technologies that are changing policing and trends that will affect future operations and practices. We are also thankful for our program managers, Zoe Mentel and Melissa Bradley, who were supportive and enthusiastic throughout the project.

We would also like to thank the law enforcement agencies that participated in our survey on the future of policing. Their responses and insights guided our research and the agenda for the executive session in Minneapolis in August 2012. And we are especially indebted to Mahogany Eller, who generously offered Target Headquarters as the location for our executive session and provided exceptional assistance in hosting the meeting.

Thanks also go to the police chiefs, scholars, and other professionals who participated in our executive session (see Appendix C for a list of participants). Many of these leaders provided a detailed look into their agencies' successes and challenges with available technologies, regional partnerships, private partnerships, multi-disciplinary collaborations, and cultural and operational trends.

Finally, credit is due to PERF staff members who conducted the survey, prepared for and hosted the executive session, and helped write and edit this report, including Jessica Toliver, David Green, Shannon Branly, Megan Collins, Kevin Greene, and Craig Fischer.

# Introduction

Police departments are far more complex than they were a generation or two ago. Though personnel are still accountable for traditional responsibilities such as calls for service and crime investigation, police have expanded their mission greatly, taking on the goals of preventing crime and reducing crime rates. Rather than focusing solely on responding to crimes after they are committed, today's best police departments are looking for ways to be proactive as well.

To identify these new proactive strategies PERF—with the support of the Office of Community Oriented Policing Services (COPS Office) and Target Corporation—conducted a *Future of Policing* survey in 2012 that was disseminated to more than 500 police agencies. Based on the nearly 200 responses received from police departments across the country, the survey results helped to identify some of the biggest opportunities and challenges that police agencies may be facing in the future.

In August of 2012 more than 30 police executives gathered at Target headquarters in Minneapolis for a day-long discussion of the survey findings and their perspectives on the state of the future of policing.[1]

Though we cannot anticipate everything that will occur in the next three to five years, we can research, survey, and discuss identified trends. We can then draw well-informed conclusions to prepare for future demands. PERF hopes that the findings reported here can help those in the field of policing adequately prepare for the coming changes.

*"Do we want to police in the future the way we are policing today? I don't think so. How did we get to where we are today? We looked; we listened; we learned; we changed; we grew with the times. That's our job as leaders today."*

–Jim Fox, Chief
Newport News, Virginia, Police Department

## Promising Crime Fighting Strategies

At the day-long meeting at Target in Minneapolis, participants engaged in discussions and provided insights into how policing could change in the next two to five years with respect to police functions and department structure, communication and the relationship between police agencies and the community, what role technology and social media will play, and how officer recruitment and retention could be affected by budget cuts.

---

1. Officials cited in this report are generally identified by their titles at the time they were quoted.

As the table below demonstrates, one significant survey finding is that a handful of policing strategies have won widespread acceptance in the law enforcement community, and predictive and intelligence-led policing appear poised to join this list in the coming years.

Table 1: PERF Survey Question: What crime fighting strategies does your agency use currently?*

| Strategy | Percentage using |
| --- | --- |
| Community policing | 94% |
| Directed patrol / focused deterrence | 94% |
| Target problem addresses / locations | 92% |
| Crime prevention programs | 91% |
| Problem-oriented policing | 89% |
| Crime mapping | 86% |
| Crime analysis | 85% |
| Regional task forces | 80% |

*Definitions of these strategies are listed in Appendix A.*

## Results Show that More Agencies Plan to Adopt Predictive Policing and Intelligence-Led Policing

The PERF survey results suggest there will be considerable growth in the practice of two strategies: predictive policing and intelligence-led policing.

**Predictive policing** was defined in a 2009 National Institute of Justice article as "taking data from disparate sources, analyzing them, and then using the results to anticipate, prevent and respond more effectively to future crime."[2] Predictive policing often begins with older strategies such as "hot spots" policing—mapping the locations where many crimes have been committed in the past. But predictive policing goes beyond hot spots policing, because it involves mining data from other sources. For example, in Arlington, Texas, police found that burglaries are more common in neighborhoods marked by physical decay. So they developed a formula for finding the most "fragile" neighborhoods. In this way, it may be possible to identify at-risk areas before they suffer a rash of burglaries or other crime.

**Intelligence-led policing** is a related concept that involves a number of factors coming together. It has been defined as "a business model and managerial philosophy where data analysis and crime intelligence are pivotal to an objective, decision-making framework that facilitates crime and problem reduction, disruption and prevention."[3] Intelligence-led policing targets prolific and serious criminal offenders in an organized, thoughtful manner.

---

2. Beth Pearsall, "Predictive Policing: The Future of Law Enforcement?" *NIJ Journal*, No. 266. www.nij.gov/journals/266/predictive.htm.
3. J.H. Ratcliffe, *Intelligence-Led Policing*, (Cullompton, Devon: Willan Publishing, 2008), http://jratcliffe.net/research/ilp.htm.

# Introduction

PERF's survey found that only 38 percent of responding police departments are currently using predictive policing, but 70 percent expect that they will implement this strategy within the next two to five years.

Similarly, 54 percent of agencies plan to implement or increase use of intelligence-led policing within the near future.

Because predictive policing and intelligence-led policing involve gathering a wide range of different types of data, they inevitably raise concerns among civil libertarians.[4] Part of the job of police executives is to anticipate such concerns and help lead a public debate about the implications of new technologies and new strategies. Furthermore, police chiefs should approach controversial strategies not merely as a process of educating the public about the police department's point of view, but also as a genuine effort to obtain community input, keep an open mind, and try to ensure that police strategies have public support.

For example, predictive policing is sometimes misinterpreted as a strategy that could target individuals before they have committed a crime. "Law enforcement should pay attention to the diversity of things that get called predictive policing," explained University of California-Los Angeles (UCLA) Professor Jeffrey Brantingham. "We need to be specific about what we are talking about when we use the term."[5]

> *"As police departments, we have gotten better at pushing down crime. Now we are looking for the thing that will take us to the next level. I firmly believe predictive policing is it."*
>
> —Charlie Beck, Chief
> Los Angeles Police Department

In California, for example, chiefs hope that predictive policing can help offset the impact of the early release of a large number of state prisoners. The early releases were prompted by a U.S. Supreme Court ruling in 2011 that found California's prisons had serious constitutional violations. The court held that prison overcrowding was causing "needless suffering and death among inmates" and upheld a lower court order mandating that the California prison system reduce its population by at least 30,000 inmates. The State of California has attempted to reduce its prison population while at the same time mitigating the risk of early release of prisoners.[6]

The Los Angeles Police Department (LAPD) is at the forefront of testing predictive policing strategies as a way to reduce crime. The development of the department's predictive policing

---

4. Martin Kaste, "Can Software that Predicts Crime Pass Constitutional Muster?" *National Public Radio* (July 26, 2013), www.npr.org/2013/07/26/205835674/can-software-that-predicts-crime-pass-constitutional-muster.
5. PERF interviews with Dr. Brantingham, who worked closely with LAPD Capt. Sean Malinowski to develop the LAPD's predictive policing program.
6. *The Early Release of Prisoners and Its Impact on Police Agencies and Communities in California.* A Joint Project of PERF and the COPS Office, May 2011, http://cops.usdoj.gov/Publications/e0811122393earlyreleaseprisoners.pdf.

tool and algorithm began in 2007 when LAPD formed a partnership with the Institute for Pure and Applied Mathematics (IPAM), a research institute housed at UCLA and funded by the National Science Foundation.[7] The relationship started informally, with LAPD Captain Sean Malinowski attending weekly meetings of the "Mathematical and Simulation Modeling of Crime" project.

During the meetings, doctoral students would present their latest crime research, and Malinowski began to see opportunities for the LAPD to use the type of analysis UCLA was using. He said, "I saw the potential of what they were doing. The LAPD didn't have the capacity for the type of analysis they were doing. They [the UCLA people] are smart people, they want to help, and they want to see how their work can have an impact in the real world. We can help them with that."

The partnership faced several barriers as it began. According to Dr. Andrea Bertozzi, Director of Applied Mathematics at UCLA, developing the predictive models required access to a large volume of detailed, accurate police data. But before the LAPD could provide the data, it had to expend significant effort to scrub the data of personal information so that it could be used in a university setting.

Bertozzi also explained it was critical to set expectations for the police department and the university early on in their partnership. "We had to establish in the beginning that we were trying to develop models that might take years to produce results that could be used in the field. Indeed, we started this project five years before anything was used in the field," Bertozzi said. Malinowski agreed, saying, "We talked a lot about how to turn the research into a tool for the field. There was a lot of trial and error."

Malinowski also said there was a give and take to ensure that both sides would get what they needed from the partnership. "We tried to design things so our partners could meet their research goals, so they could get a scientific benefit out of it. That involves some sacrifice on our end," he said. "But it was also important for them to recognize that we are working in an environment with real-world consequences, so we need real-world solutions."

LAPD's predictive policing development team considered using various commercially available products before eventually deciding to use an algorithm developed at UCLA. (An algorithm is a step-by-step procedure for solving a problem or accomplishing some end, especially by a computer.)

LAPD's algorithm processes updates crime data in "near-real time" and produces crime forecasts twice each day. The algorithm draws on seven years of crime data to produce forecasts for burglary, burglary from a motor vehicle, and vehicle thefts. These crimes best

---

7. www.ipam.ucla.edu/news.aspx

fit the theoretical models that the algorithm is based on. The program is used for property crimes because "criminologists have found that property crime is a predictable act that can be deterred simply by having a police presence in the area, but violent crime is harder to predict and deter."[8]

Currently, LAPD's predictive policing program is being applied to a 50-square-mile area. The program breaks up the larger area into a grid composed of 500-foot squares, or "boxes." Each forecast assigns a crime probability score to each box. Patrol officers are informed of the highest probability boxes and are directed to use any available time to focus on those boxes. "Our mantra is in their available time, officers should 'get in the box,'" Malinowski said. The department encourages officers to proactively use their knowledge, skills, and experience to identify reasons why the box has a high crime risk and then actively work to address those issues.

> **COMPUTERS WILL NOT MAKE HUMAN ANALYSIS OBSOLETE**
>
> LAPD had to answer questions from employees, especially analysts, who thought the software would make their job unnecessary.
>
> Captain Malinowski says, "I told them, if I can automate targeting and tasking for patrol, I can have you do deeper analysis about problem locations. I have a million things for analysts to do."

For law enforcement leaders who are interested in implementing predictive policing, LAPD Deputy Chief Pat Gannon outlines several suggestions. "It will work as long as the officers understand that it's not about just going into the box," he said. "We have to be more sophisticated than that. It's about having a mission once you get into the box, and developing strategies to achieve the mission."

Gannon also stresses it is important to obtain officers' buy-in for the program. "If we send the cops out on a mission without talking to them and getting their input, we're not going to be successful," he said. "The process leading into the implementation is very important. There has to be a tremendous amount of work done to ensure everyone understands what it's all about."

*"I believe predictive policing is an important tool that can aid police departments in the deployment of limited resources. I hope it will become part of standard technology used by law enforcement agencies."*

—Dr. Andrea Bertozzi
UCLA Mathematician

Brantingham points out that predictive analytics will not replace officer skills. The software is capable of highlighting where and when crime is likely to take place, but officers must then determine how to disrupt the criminal opportunity.

---

8. Dana Mackenzie, "Predictive Policing," *Society for Industrial and Applied Mathematics* (March 16, 2012), www.siam.org/news/news.php?id=1953.

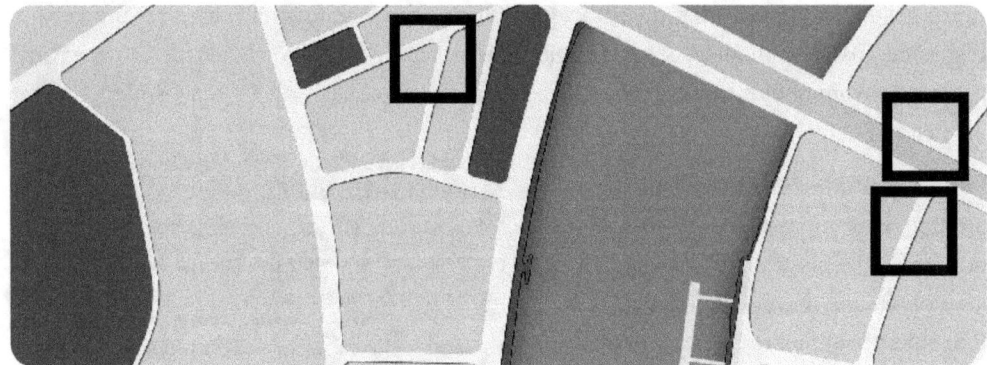

Malinowski said he explains the program to his officers as a way to play the probabilities to fight crime. "Using this data will allow them to deny criminals the opportunity to commit a crime," he said. "But when they spend time in the high-probability areas, they need to be doing problem solving. There is something there that is attracting criminals; we tell officers to look for the magnets. What are they, and how can they be mitigated? The goal isn't more arrests, the goal is crime prevention."

It is too early to conclusively assess the effectiveness of LAPD's predictive policing program, but early results are promising. To assess the tool, LAPD completed a six-month randomized experiment that pitted the predictive policing algorithm against human crime analysts using all of the other tools at their disposal. The designers of the experiment hoped to find that the predictive policing tool was as effective as a human analyst, since that would free analysts to work on other types of investigation and analysis.

The initial results showed that the algorithm consistently predicted the location of future crimes twice as accurately as human analysts were able to do. The test areas experienced crime declines, and there does not appear to be a crime "displacement" occurring, said Gannon.

Moving forward, LAPD hopes to use predictive policing in more geographic areas and for violent and gang-related crime. Academics who have worked on the project say they would also like to expand the data set the program uses to include more variables, such as patterns of truancy, land use, and vacant housing. They would also like to study the relationships between different types of crimes, analyze networks of gang rivalries, and develop more sophisticated mapping capabilities.[10]

The Albuquerque Police Department is also using predictive analytics. "We use graduated, color maps, which depict where property crimes are likely to occur," said Chief Ray Schultz.

---

10. PERF staff correspondence with Dr. Andrea Bertozzi, March 2013.

Introduction

Once a high-risk area is identified, officers are encouraged to spend more time in the area. Albuquerque police have taken this a step farther; in certain cases, "bait" cars or other items are placed in targeted locations identified through the predictive analytics program. (Bait items have included everything from iPads to large spools of copper wire.) When a bait item is stolen, the police department sometimes tracks the item before making an arrest, in order to determine where stolen items are being taken and/or sold. Thus, police can not only apprehend the individual suspect, but dismantle an entire fencing operation. The department has recovered a large amount of stolen property through these tracking efforts and gained information about these larger illicit networks.

## Considerations for Appropriate Use of Predictive Policing Strategies

At PERF's Future Trends in Policing Summit, Madison, Wisconsin, Police Chief Noble Wray discussed possible unintended consequences resulting from efforts to be more efficient and accountable. If police managers closely prescribe where officers should spend every moment and tell them precisely what they need to do, it may stifle officers' creativity and innovation, he said.

Wray asked, "What will it do to [an] officer's ability to think outside the box if we tighten our control of them too much? Our future leaders need to be innovative, so I wonder if we are tightening the directives a little too much."

Bob Lunney, law enforcement consultant and former chief of several large police departments in Canada, also sees a risk of micromanaging officers: "If predictive analytics are perceived as dictating an officer's activity, officers may resent that they are not being given enough autonomy, or they may feel that the department is not treating them as intelligent professionals."

Gannon, however, pointed out that predictive analytics should be used only as an aid for officers. Predictive analytics is not mutually exclusive with problem solving by officers, he said. In fact, officers are instructed and continuously encouraged to use their problem-solving abilities.

> *"We need to be very eloquent about articulating our policing philosophy. We need to inculcate that philosophy into every officer in the department.*
>
> *"We also need broader policies. We have a tendency to write a new policy every time something goes wrong, hoping it won't happen again. But doing that results in a web of policies that are so demanding that we strip the front line officer of a lot of the discretion they are intended to have under a modern democratic policing system."*
>
> —Robert F. Lunney
> Author of *Parting Shots: My Passion for Policing*

## HOW CAN POLICE TAKE HOT SPOTS ENFORCEMENT TO THE NEXT LEVEL?

*By Dr. David Weisburd,*
*Director of the Center for Evidence-Based Crime Policy, George Mason University*

Empirical evidence has become an important part of policing. Perhaps more than any other part of the criminal justice system, evidence-based policy has taken hold in policing, and the police are looking to researchers to help them in defining which policies and practices they should adopt.

The National Research Council has argued that the strongest evidence for police effectiveness has come from studies of policing at hot spots. What is the evidence?

A series of studies show that crime is very concentrated in urban areas. Indeed, there seems to be a law of crime concentrations in urban areas. In my own research I have found that in Seattle, New York, Sacramento, and Tel Aviv, between 4 and 5 percent of the street segments in a city, intersection to intersection, produce 50 percent of crime.

In Seattle, we found that almost the exact same level of concentration of crime existed year to year across 16 years, irrespective of a declining crime trend in the period studied. And just one percent of the streets in Seattle experienced consistently high crime rates during this period, producing almost 25 percent of Seattle's crime.

Importantly, such crime hot spots are not concentrated in a single area, but are spread throughout the city. There are hot spots in so-called "good neighborhoods," and most streets have very little crime even in so called "bad neighborhoods."

This law of crime concentrations led Lawrence Sherman, Director of the University of Cambridge's Institute of Criminology, and I to conduct a large randomized field study of hot spots policing, based on Sherman's finding that most crime calls in Minneapolis were concentrated at a relatively small number of street addresses. Randomly allocating police patrol to crime hot spots, we found that the police could significantly reduce crime on the streets that received hot spots patrol. Our findings were in stark contrast to the prevailing assumption among scholars in the early 1990s that the police could not prevent crime.

Subsequent research has confirmed our findings. Rutgers University Professor Anthony Braga and his colleagues identified 21 hot spot field tests, and found that 19 produced significant crime prevention benefits. And there is little evidence of displacement to areas nearby; crime does not simply "move around the corner." In fact, there is strong evidence today that areas nearby are most likely to *improve* as a result of hot spots policing programs.

**Based on this research, I have argued that the police must refocus their paradigm of crime control from one that is centered on offenders to one that is centered on places.**

By putting an emphasis on reducing opportunities for crime at places, not on waiting for crimes to occur and then arresting offenders, place-based policing offers an approach to crime prevention that can increase public safety while decreasing the human and financial costs of imprisonment for Americans. If place-based policing were to become the central focus of police, rather than the arrest and apprehension of offenders, then we likely would see a reduction of prison populations as well as an increase in the crime-prevention effectiveness of the police.

Chief Michael Davis, from Brooklyn Park, Minnesota, and I have recently added a new dimension to the promise of hot spots policing. Based on a recent study in which we found many social as well as opportunity-based risk factors for chronic crime hot spots, Davis and I have begun to argue for policing that increases "collective efficacy"[10] and informal social controls at crime hot spots. The focus on crime hot spots provides an opportunity to reduce the scale of social and health interventions. Just as efficiency in patrol can be increased by directing police at chronic crime hot spots, it may also be possible to create greater efficiency in social interventions.

**In other words, trying to increase collective efficacy and community social controls across a whole neighborhood may simply be too large a task for police and other crime prevention agents. But focusing on just one percent of the city streets may make such interventions realistic.**

The evidence-based future of policing must include a focus on the small percentage of streets that generate much of the crime in a city. But that focus will be most effective if the police try to use not only strategies that increase surveillance and deterrence, but also ones that try to strengthen the micro-communities of people who live in crime hot spots.

---

10. Harvard Professor Robert Sampson and his colleagues define collective efficacy as "social cohesion among neighbors combined with their willingness to intervene on behalf of the common good."

# Tailoring Partnerships to Maximize Public Safety

PERF's survey of police departments regarding future-oriented trends found that 94 percent of survey respondents already partner with other police agencies to increase coordination of their crime fighting strategies. There was strong agreement at the PERF Summit among police chiefs that partnerships will remain a key strategy in coming years, for a number of reasons.

> **SURVEY RESULTS**
>
> 50% of agencies provide a specialized function (e.g., SWAT, aviation, or forensics) to another agency.
>
> 80% of agencies participate on regional teams, units, or task forces.

First, the economic crisis of 2008 began a process of budget cutting in many police departments that has lasted for years. Budget cutting has abated in some jurisdictions, but the cutbacks left most police chiefs with an appreciation for the fragility of their funding. Partnerships can serve as an efficient, cost-saving way for departments to share the costs of certain functions while combining the skills of multiple departments.

Furthermore, partnerships are part of the very definition of community policing:

Community policing is a philosophy that promotes organizational strategies, which support the systematic use of partnerships and problem-solving techniques, to proactively address the immediate conditions that give rise to public safety issues such as crime, social disorder, and fear of crime.[11]

Table 2: PERF Survey Question: What partnerships does your agency currently use?

| Partnership | Percentage using |
| --- | --- |
| Other local law enforcement agencies | 94% |
| Non-profit or non-governmental organization | 80% |
| Businesses/corporations | 69% |
| Other private organizations | 54% |
| Police foundations | 46% |
| Private security companies | 34% |

In this chapter, we will describe a number of types of partnerships that law enforcement agencies have found productive and helpful.

---

11. *Community Policing Defined* (Washington, DC: Office of Community Oriented Policing Services, 2012, 3). http://ric-zai-inc.com/Publications/cops-p157-pub.pdf.

# Police Foundations: A Promising Partnership to Help Bridge Funding Gaps

As departments across the country struggled in recent years with budget cuts, some turned to police foundations as a way to bolster funding. According to Pam Delaney, Director of the National Police Foundations Project, police foundations are defined as "nonprofit organizations that help raise money and provide resources for police programs, equipment, and special needs that cannot be readily provided through public sector funds."

Delaney said foundations not only offer a "promising source to help bridge funding gaps," but they can also help business leaders to become active partners in crime prevention and community safety. For example, some corporations have opened up their leadership training to police officers, shared their expertise, or provided law enforcement with access to equipment, technology, meeting space, and other resources.

The National Police Foundations Project was launched in September 2010 with support from the COPS Office and Target. The number of police foundations nationwide has grown rapidly. There are currently 180 foundations, which represents a 20 percent increase over two years ago. There are also approximately 35 sheriffs' foundations and 25 to 40 state police foundations. The growth in police foundations has been assisted by the National Police Foundations Project,[12] which has held regional workshops to help departments create or expand foundations. The project is working on establishing a formal association of police foundations—including a website where representatives from different foundations can network and learn from each other—and developing an online "start-up guide" for departments that are interested in starting their own foundation.

During workshops that were held by the National Police Foundations Project, police leaders often reported facing comparable challenges. For example, a common challenge was identifying private-sector leaders with whom to partner. Ideally, the private-sector partners should be passionate about helping the police department and should be willing to help lead the foundation.

Even after potential partners are identified, many chiefs struggle with how to present the idea to private-sector leaders, as there is a natural reluctance to approach people and ask for something. Some chiefs worry that private-sector partners will think there is some type of "quid pro quo" involved, and making the initial approach asking for a partnership can be uncomfortable. Delaney pointed out that for chiefs, "Getting the right board members is the biggest challenge. Chiefs have to strategize about the right people to approach, how to actually recruit them, and how to empower them as spokespeople for the foundation. They

---

12. Further information about the National Police Foundations Project is available online at www.cops.usdoj.gov/html/dispatch/06-2011/NationalPoliceFoundationsProject.asp.

> **A STRONG PRIVATE-SECTOR PARTNERSHIP: TARGET CORPORATION**
>
> In the mid-1990s, crime rates in Minneapolis, where Target Corporation is headquartered, increased substantially. Target's then-CEO Bob Ulrich read an article about a repeat criminal who raped a woman after he was mistakenly released from custody due to an information-sharing failure. Ulrich decided that supporting law enforcement would be a priority for Target.
>
> Today, one way in which Target supports police is by sharing its forensic video analysis expertise. Investigators at Target's forensics laboratory, which is accredited by the American Society of Crime Laboratory Directors/ Laboratory Accreditation Board, spend nearly half their time providing assistance to law enforcement agencies. According to FBI Special Agent Paul McCabe, Target has "one of the nation's top forensics labs." In one early case, Target's assistance with video analysis was critical to solving a homicide in Houston. Word of Target's forensic capabilities and assistance spread, and as demand for assistance increased, Target decided to focus on providing assistance in cases involving violent felonies.

have to find someone outside of the department who can take the ball and run with it. That is when police foundations will best succeed."

Despite the initial challenges, Delaney said, "After the first one or two partners are recruited, it becomes much easier, since current board members can help recruit new ones. Police foundations don't usually get started rapidly, but once they are established they can be an invaluable ally. You will have a group of influential people in the community who will understand the complexities of policing, so that when issues develop, you have a group of people who can help you achieve your goals for the police department."

Delaney, who previously served as president of the New York City Police Foundation, along with directors of police foundations in other cities have developed guidance for avoiding conflicts of interest or other problems with police foundations.[13] It is important to avoid any connection with political activity and to have written conflict-of-interest policies for board members, they noted. And because policing involves the public trust in ways that other institutions do not, certain fundraising strategies commonly used elsewhere—such as naming a facility for a donor—clearly are not acceptable for police foundations.

## Building Partnerships with Federal Law Enforcement Agencies

Partnerships with federal law enforcement agencies can complement operations and serve as a cost-saving mechanism for local agencies. At PERF's Summit, Sharon Lubinski, the United States Marshal for the District of Minnesota, discussed the various partnerships the U.S. Marshals Service maintains with local law enforcement agencies, including fugitive and sex offender task forces. In certain cases the Marshals are even able to provide support to local task force participants in the form of overtime or vehicles.

---

13. "Foundations Help to Fund Innovation and Creativity in Policing," *Subject to Debate*, a PERF newsletter, May 2008, www.washingtonpost.com/wp-dyn/content/article/2006/01/28/AR2006012801268.html.

In Camden, New Jersey, a financially strapped city that laid off nearly half its police force in 2011, Police Chief Scott Thomson decided on a strategy of tapping into federal partnerships to keep the rest of the department functioning. The Camden Police Department works closely with the FBI, DEA, ATF, U.S. Marshals Service, county prosecutors, and the New Jersey State Police. To give the partners a place to collaborate, Thomson used forfeiture funds to lease 15,000 square feet of office space, and the partners meet once every few weeks to discuss the latest crime patterns, potential responses, and to leverage the knowledge, skills, and resources of all participants to effectively investigate cases and respond to events.

The FBI's Regional Forensics Computer Labs (RFCL) are another key resource. These facilities are described as "a one stop, full service forensics laboratory and training center devoted entirely to the examination of digital evidence in support of criminal investigations."[14] These RFCLs combine the expertise of federal, state, and local law enforcement and universities.

Albuquerque Police Chief Ray Schultz said the RFCL in his city has helped solve crimes and improve homicide clearance rates. If the victim of a violent crime has a cell phone, the police department takes that phone to the RCFL, which can gather investigative data from the phone. "In most homicides, one of the previous three calls on the victim's phone will be either to or from the offender," Schultz said. "The RFCL can create and provide to investigators a 'clone' of the data on the phone, including call history, text message history, and other saved contents."

## Partnerships with Universities and Other Researchers: Potential Growth Area for the Future

Despite the proven benefits of collaboration between law enforcement agencies and researchers, PERF's survey found that only 9 percent of responding agencies had any type of partnership with university-based researchers. Chief Kim Dine of Frederick, Maryland, said that police departments are missing a valuable opportunity and resource if they are not working with local universities. Dine likened police departments to "living laboratories" with huge volumes of data, but police are not always able to harness the information in a useful way. Universities may be able to help departments analyze their data so that it may be more productively utilized. One example of this by the Frederick Police Department was a study completed at Dine's request by criminal justice students at Mount St. Mary's University to assess the value and efficacy of Frederick's Police Activities League program. This effort resulted in a valuable resource that enabled the department to explain the value of the program to stakeholders and city leaders. The Frederick Police Department has also been very proactive about using college interns, who help enhance the agency's ability to combat crime while maximizing the effectiveness of personnel.

---

14. "About RCFLs," Regional Computer Forensics Laboratory, www.rcfl.gov/DSP_P_about.cfm.

Partnerships with a police agency can offer many benefits to researchers, especially access to data. Professors also may find that a working relationship with a police department provides internship opportunities for the professor's students and access to police officials who are willing to serve as guest lecturers or to provide real-world perspectives on the professor's courses on policing.[15]

The National Institute of Justice has identified factors that lead to success in locally initiated research partnerships:

- Partners must develop good working relationships
- Trust between the partners must be cultivated
- Researchers should invest in understanding the police culture
- Graduate students can be used effectively
- Information systems must be able to support research
- Key staff must remain in place[16]

Joshua Ederheimer, Acting Director of the COPS Office, urged law enforcement to consider forming research partnerships. As an example of innovative thinking about partnerships, Ederheimer pointed to New Haven, Connecticut, Police Chief Dean Esserman's idea of forming "teaching" police departments. Esserman has noted that while there are thousands of hospitals in the United States, there are only about 200 "teaching hospitals" affiliated with medical schools. He has called for police departments to adopt this concept, in which certain departments would serve both as operational police departments and as an environment to provide ongoing education to future and current police officers. "The commitment is to lifelong learning," Esserman said.[17]

Dine described a successful partnership between police and the Maryland Network Against Domestic Violence (MNADV), a state coalition of domestic violence prevention experts and service providers. Police from a number of departments in Maryland and the MNADV developed a series of research-based questions for police officers to ask victims at the scene of a domestic violence incident. The Frederick Police Department was chosen to represent all municipal agencies in the state, and with other agencies representing county departments and sheriffs' offices, the questions were tested for what ultimately became a statewide effort to combat domestic violence.

---

15. Beth A. Sanders and Marc L. Fields, "Partnerships with University-Based Researchers," *The Police Chief*, June 2009, www.policechiefmagazine.org/magazine/index.cfm?fuseaction=display_arch&article_id=1821&issue_id=62009.
16. Tom McEwen, "NIJ's Locally Initiated Research Partnerships in Policing: Factors That Add up to Success," *National Institute of Justice Journal* (January 1999), www.ilj.org/publications/docs/NIJs_Locally_Initiated_Research_Partnerships.pdf.
17. "Transcript: Innovations in Policing—Innovation Behind the Teaching Police Department: An Interview with Colonel Dean Esserman," by James H. Burch II, Bureau of Justice Assistance, podcast audio, https://www.bja.gov/publications/podcasts/multimedia/transcript/Transcript_Esserman_508.pdf.
    See also "Teaching Police Department Initiative: Creating a New Paradigm for Police Leadership," Roger Williams University, *Justice System Training and Research Institute News*, Winter 2011, www.rwu.edu/sites/default/files/justice11.pdf.

The answers that officers receive result in a "lethality assessment"—a measurement of the victim's risk of suffering death or serious injury at the hands of their intimate partner.

Victims who are found to be at high risk of death or serious injury are immediately connected with a domestic violence service provider. Dine believes that this lethality assessment is a model approach that other agencies and states should adopt to help reduce domestic violence crime.

The lethality assessment program is grounded in research that found that victims of domestic violence often underestimate the degree of danger their partners pose to them. Furthermore, research shows that victims who take advantage of domestic violence services have a substantially lower risk of suffering a serious attack than those who do not receive the services. While it cannot be conclusively linked to the lethality assessment program, Maryland has experienced a 41 percent decline in intimate partner homicides during a three-year period while the program was in effect.[18]

> **CAN VENTURING OUTSIDE TRADITIONAL AREAS OF RESPONSIBILITY LEAD TO TRANSFORMATIONAL CRIME REDUCTIONS?**
>
> I'm a strong proponent of law enforcement venturing outside of our traditional swimming lane. We can partner with schools, other cities, and additional partners to deal with issues that are outside the traditional purview of the police, but which impact crime.
>
> It's heavy, difficult work, but it's the work we can do that will be transformational. Delivering good immediate police response is important, but its impact is ephemeral, and we can do more. I believe our primary role is to achieve crime reduction. I want permanent improvements.
>
> Doctors alone can't take care of our health, schools alone cannot educate our kids, and the police alone cannot ensure safety.
>
> —Michael Davis, Chief
> Brooklyn Park, Minnesota, Police Department

## Albuquerque Police Partner with Business Groups and Sandia National Laboratories

In recent years, the Albuquerque Police Department (APD) has worked with business organizations in a variety of fields to help them share information with each other and with the police about patterns of criminal activity and suspects. Retail stores, construction-related businesses, and hotels and motels are among the groups that now share information with each other and the police in real time via the Internet.

For example, the Albuquerque Retail Asset Protection Association (ARAPA) is comprised of law enforcement and private sector partners who share information about retail thefts. Often, the information consists of security camera footage of suspects involved in thefts or

---

18. "Lethality Assessment Program: Maryland Model for First Responders—Learning to Read the Danger Signs." Bowie, MD: Maryland Network Against Domestic Violence, http://mnadv.org/_mnadvWeb/wp-content/uploads/2011/10/LAP_Info_Packet--as_of_12-8-10.pdf.

fraudulent transactions. Because organized criminal groups sometimes come to Albuquerque for a short period of time to commit a quick series of crimes, the real-time information shared through ARAPA helps stores to be on the lookout for suspects who have been identified by other members of the association. Karen Fischer, an APD employee who helps manage ARAPA, said that members of the group have established a strong level of trust about sharing sensitive information with each other. The information is available to ARAPA members through a secure web portal.[19]

## WORKING WITH SANDIA NATIONAL LABORATORIES

The APD also has developed an important partnership with the Sandia National Laboratories, whose primary facilities are located in Albuquerque. Sandia National Laboratories is operated and managed by Sandia Corporation, a wholly owned subsidiary of Lockheed Martin Corporation. Sandia Corporation operates Sandia National Laboratories as a contractor for the U.S. Department of Energy's National Nuclear Security Administration (NNSA) and supports numerous federal, state, and local government agencies, companies, and organizations. For more than 20 years, scientists from Sandia have donated their time to collaborate with the police department as part of Sandia's community service efforts. Chief Schultz of Albuquerque stated that "One of the priorities for the labs is finding out whether tools and technology that have been developed for the military can help civilian law enforcement agencies."

*"Our real time crime center will allow officers to access school cameras if an emergency call is received from a school, and officers are working with private sector partners to allow the department to access their camera systems in the event of an emergency."*

—Raymond Schultz, Chief
Albuquerque Police Department

In one major project, Sandia scientists helped the police establish a Real Time Crime Center that quickly provides information to officers in the field. When police receive a high-risk call, a team of analysts works quickly—within minutes—to provide officers with any information that could help resolve the call safely. The information that analysts find is delivered to the officers' mobile data terminals and their smart phones. The information might include mapping or floor plans of the location of the call, criminal histories of residents at the address, any restraining orders, prior contacts with law enforcement, and whether anyone involved poses a safety risk to an officer. "We are trying to quantify exactly how important this additional information is for officers," Schultz said. "There is a whole team of Ph.D.'s working on this."

Further information about ARAPA is available at www.policeforum.org/library/safe-cities/Target_Safe%20City.pdf.

## CHIEF MICHAEL DAVIS FOCUSES ON RESEARCH ABOUT STRONG COMMUNITIES

The Brooklyn Park, Minnesota, Police Department has established successful research partnerships under the leadership of Chief Michael Davis.

Davis acknowledges that there are barriers to effective collaboration. "I believe strongly in the importance of good research. But there is a lot of 'group-think' in law enforcement, and not a lot of reaching out to academic people. And there aren't many academics reaching out to law enforcement," he said. And even when police chiefs recognize the benefits of a research partnership, "The realities of being a police chief catch up to folks," Davis said. "We can have a thoughtful discussion with researchers about crime prevention, but meanwhile chiefs might have a city council or mayor who thinks the police department should focus only on enforcement."

Davis is especially interested in research about what creates thriving communities. He is applying concepts developed by researchers to "leverage assets in the community to build a sense of collective ownership that is both powerful and sustainable. It's about more than putting cops on dots. We need to appreciate the complexity of the problem in locations where violence is endemic. Social norms, social structures, absence of typical family structures, low community connectivity, and high transiency all play a role."

"Collective efficacy" requires people living in a certain area to know and trust one another. Davis encourages this by convening community meetings in which residents are organized into small discussion groups to talk about the future and how to improve their neighborhood.

Meetings can take many forms, but Davis says the important thing is that "police need to be the community conveners. We can help create new relationships. Police department employees are usually the most talented, versatile, innovative people in city government, so police chiefs should harness their employees to build relationships. Your employees have the acumen to do it."

Davis discussed one example of a community meeting that helped build neighborhood ties. Partnering with staff from the city's Parks and Recreation Department, police went into distressed neighborhoods at around the time when residents were arriving home from work. "We visited their neighborhood with a 'park in a bag,' which is a bag provided by Parks and Rec that is filled with toys and games for children. As the adults arrived home, we would invite them to talk with us, and while we spoke with the adults the Parks and Rec staff engaged the kids with the toys and games. We were discussing a burglary problem in the neighborhood, but we were also introducing neighbors to each other, getting them talking. When we do this type of thing, they feel like we are looking out for them, and we are being proactive."

Source: PERF Phone conference with Chief Michael Davis.

The department also is developing a network of "smart boards"—video screens in briefing rooms that display automated information, including predictive crime models, information about offenders being released back into the community, and recent arrest information. Schultz describes it as "like having a 24-hour CNN news network."

> **CONSIDERATIONS FOR DEVELOPING POLICE PARTNERSHIPS WITH ACADEMIA**
> Both academics and the police can take steps to improve research relationships.
>
> Academics tend to have an overly enthusiastic sense of the importance of their work. Often they don't focus on practical utility. Academics need to think about their work and ask, "Will this disrupt the work of the police? Has it been tailored for law enforcement use?"
>
> I didn't think of these questions when I first started working with police, but over time I have developed an appreciation for the fact that new tools have to fit comfortably within the policing environment. If the tools we develop make the officer's job harder, they won't use it, so we need to develop tools that work seamlessly in an officer's environment. Researchers also need to recognize that policing is a person-intensive business; it is ultimately about the officers, their judgment, and how they work.
>
> For the police, it can be difficult to take a long-term orientation toward research. In my research with LAPD, I was lucky that the department knew the research wouldn't lead to immediate results, and they were okay with that, but undertaking long-term research projects is a very difficult decision for police departments. Police are responsible for dealing with crime in the here and now, so academics should try to help by developing research and tools that are useful on a practical, day-to-day level.
>
> I think it would work to the advantage of police agencies if they adopt a more experimental mindset. There are many academic ideas out there and many vendors who would like to sell their products to the police, but without experimentation it's hard to know which ideas work and which do not. There are costs and risks associated with experiments, but the benefits far outweigh the risks. Law enforcement might follow the example of the pharmaceutical industry, which routinely completes trials to determine whether new drugs work better than existing remedies. Evidence based medicine is better than superstition, and the same concept applies to policing.
>
> —Dr. Jeffrey Brantingham<br>UCLA Professor and LAPD Partner

Sandia scientists are also donating time to work on improving the use of facial recognition software. In New Mexico, all state driver's license photos are entered into a facial recognition database. Police can compare images from surveillance footage with the photos to identify suspects. This practice has become more effective as the quality of surveillance footage has gradually improved, and officers are currently able to identify about 30 percent of suspects who appear in surveillance footage by using facial recognition, according to Schultz.

Albuquerque police and Sandia have collaborated on many other projects. One project developed and tested counter-explosives technology, including the Percussion Actuated Non-Electric (PAN) explosives disruptor, which is designed to remotely disable and render safe improvised explosives devices. The PAN is now being used by departments around the world. Another project explored how to use three-dimensional laser mapping to document crime scenes. Rather than using tape measures in recording a crime scene, police can use inputs from cameras and 3D sensors to create a graphical model of the scene.[20]

## A Partnership between Police and Pawn Shops to Reduce Theft

Chief Kim Jacobs of the Columbus, Ohio, Police Department reported on a partnership that her department has developed with one element of the business community: pawn shops and scrap yards. The goal is to reduce thefts by targeting burglars and thieves who are repeat offenders.

The city compiled a computerized "do-not-buy" list of more than 22,000 individuals who have been convicted of theft or a theft-related offense in Columbus or surrounding areas within the past six years.[21] The city shares the electronic list quarterly with scrap yards and pawn shops, which are prohibited from purchasing goods from anyone on the list. Anyone caught purchasing goods from someone on the "do-not-buy" list can be charged with a misdemeanor and owners could lose their business license.[22]

---

20. For additional information, see Charles Q. Little et al., "Forensic 3D Scene Reconstruction," *SPIE Applied Imagery Pattern Recognition Workshop,* October 1999, www.osti.gov/bridge/servlets/purl/13967-Gey0Ey/webviewable/13967.pdf.
21. Columbus City Council, "Columbus Thwarting Theft with Twelvefold Expansion of Do-Not-Buy List," media release, May 8, 2012, http://council.columbus.gov/advrel_content.aspx?id=51578.
22. At the time of this writing, Jacobs and her department were analyzing results and did not have any further data to share with us.

**SURVEY RESULTS: TYPES OF ORGANIZATIONS WITH POLICE PARTNERSHIPS**
- Rotary Club
- Lions Club
- Mothers Against Drunk Driving
- United Way
- Child Advocacy Centers
- Department of Health
- Department of Corrections
- Schools/Universities
- Local Chamber of Commerce

In addition to working with business owners, Columbus police had to work closely with court officials in several jurisdictions to obtain the lists of convicted thieves.

Many police agencies responding to PERF's survey about future strategies reported that they are deploying a wide variety of technological advances to improve services, and in some cases to save money.

**Table 3:** PERF Survey Question: In the next two to five years, do you anticipate an increase in the following strategies?

| Strategy | Percentage of agencies |
|---|---|
| Online crime reporting | 82% |
| 911 dispatchers sending/receiving text messages | 74% |
| Telephone crime reporting | 61% |
| "Reverse 911" to disseminate messages from police | 60% |
| Allowing crime victims to check their case status online | 59% |
| Non-sworn response to certain calls for service | 57% |

## Reducing Police Response to Minor Crimes

The economic crisis of 2008 caused many police departments across the country to look for ways of saving money, and many considered whether they can afford to continue responding to all of the different types of calls for service. PERF's "Future Trends in Policing" survey showed that most departments are moving toward online crime reporting and eliminating response by sworn officers to certain types of calls for service.

One common area that is often mentioned as a possibility for reduced police response is thefts, burglaries, vandalism, or other crimes that were committed hours before the victim calls the police. For example, people return home from work or from being out of town and find their house has been broken into, or a bicycle has been stolen from their back yard. The theft probably occurred hours or even days before it was discovered. Is it an effective use of police officers' time to respond to such a call?

There is not a yes-or-no answer to that question. Some police officials acknowledge that it is unlikely that officers responding to such calls will find evidence that could lead to a burglary suspect being identified and convicted. But at the same time they realize that victims may feel traumatized, and victims like to have the opportunity to speak to a police officer about it. So police leaders are cautious about making any abrupt changes in response policies without having a sense of whether their communities will support the changes.

Dr. George Kelling of Rutgers University, co-author of the landmark "broken windows" approach to policing, argues that new ways of thinking are needed about police response to calls for service. In Kelling's view, scaling back the fast response of sworn officers to minor crime scenes should not be proposed as a budget-cutting strategy, but rather as a strategy to improve the effectiveness of policing. The more time that police officers spend responding to minor theft calls, the less time they have available for effective, pro-active initiatives such as problem solving, he explained. And rushing to crime scenes when a fast response is not needed is wasteful.

"We have to de-market 911 and make people understand that 911 is a low payoff strategy," Kelling said. "This doesn't mean I think the police should never rush to a scene. At times they should rush. But we should not withhold police services—we should not de-police city streets—in the name of rapid response times."

Unfortunately, rapid response to 911 calls is "a bad idea that is intuitively reasonable" to the public, Kelling said. Residents of a community tend to think they have an excellent police department if officers respond within minutes to any type of call, no matter how minor.

"So we must be especially clever in developing arguments that will convince the general public that it is not a good idea to send cars constantly, repeatedly, to calls that we know will not make any difference," Kelling said.

> *"It's a real challenge. When we don't respond to certain calls, we do lose an opportunity. These types of calls are our bread and butter interactions with the community. But I think there are other ways to interact with the community more efficiently."*
>
> –Chris Moore, Chief
> San Jose, California, Police Department

Chief Scott Thomson of the Camden Police Department can attest to the increased efficiency experienced by implementing this strategy. His department faced a massive challenge when he lost approximately half his police force due to city budget cuts. (Later, the city police department was replaced by a new county agency with increased funding and staffing.)

Faced with the need to make sharp, immediate cuts, Thomson made a number of major changes, including altering how the department responds to calls for service:

> *After our decrease in personnel, there were things we could no longer do. By cutting some services, we could focus on doing critical functions more efficiently and more effectively. Specifically, we stopped responding to property crimes unless they were in-progress or there were other pressing safety concerns. There wasn't a tremendous pushback from the community when we did that, because we got them on board with it before implementation.*

> *As a result of the changes, we were able to cut our response times to priority-one calls in half, even with only half of our police department. That's also because we were utilizing technology, but it's mostly attributable to not burdening our officers with going to every single call for service. We ended the age-old guarantee that we will send a cop to EVERY call.*

The San Jose Police Department also experienced a reduction in force, which caused the department to reevaluate how it responded to calls. "We found that burglar alarm calls without verification were our second most common type of call, and 98 percent of them were false alarms," Chief Chris Moore said. He decided that responding to unverified alarm calls was not a good use of department resources. "You can't make these decisions lightly, but you have to prioritize," Moore said.

In some cities, residents reporting relatively minor crimes are directed to file a crime report online, rather than having an officer respond to the scene and taking a report. This can ensure that the crime is recorded for purposes of calculating crime rates, without requiring an officer to spend time taking down information that the victim can provide directly. And the computerized system can generate a crime report number that victims can provide to their insurance companies.

Some police chiefs have pointed out that many people are accustomed to doing things online, such as shopping, banking, and paying bills. For some people, filing a crime report online about a minor offense is easier than calling police and waiting for an officer to respond and take a report manually. Police departments increasingly are placing "Report a Crime" buttons on their homepages for this purpose.

Moore said that if you maintain communication with residents about these types of changes in police services, "Most people understand that there are ways to get them the information they need from police online, quickly and accurately."

At PERF's Summit, several chiefs expressed concerns about scaling back the police response to residents. Chief Michael Davis of Brooklyn Park, Minnesota, acknowledged that in some places, informal social controls have atrophied, so citizens become over-reliant on the police. "Most of our calls have nothing to do with reportable crime, which indicates an overreliance on the police," he said. But Davis said he thinks responding to these calls is important because the police response is an opportunity to build trust with the community.

## Additional Cost Saving Strategies for Consideration

Consolidating city agencies may be another cost saving measure considered by city managers or elected officials. However, PERF's survey found that law enforcement leaders think the drawbacks of consolidation outweigh the benefits, with 71 percent of responding agencies stating that they oppose mergers of police and fire departments. Chiefs believe that the culture and skills of law enforcement and fire departments are significantly different, which may prevent effective integration. Some chiefs believe that consolidation of EMS and fire services would be a better fit.

### ACCOUNTABILITY

Bob Cherry, President of Baltimore's Fraternal Order of Police and a detective with the Baltimore Police Department, argued that departments should focus on the quality of police officers rather than the quantity:

> *"Solving our problems isn't always about having more cops. It's about raising standards and advancing to the next level. Some cities may need more police, but we should also concentrate on building a leaner, smarter, more professional police force.*
>
> *We should focus on hiring officers who will meet our best standards and who will work well and produce. And then we need to hold everyone accountable."*

Chief Tim Dolan of Minneapolis added that more stringent hiring standards and increased accountability may also improve the level of pride in an agency, which can have cascading beneficial effects. For example, a greater degree of pride could help reduce officer turnover and the number of officers out on suspension, medical leave, and/or light duty, he said.

## Private Security and Off-Duty Employment: Opportunities and Challenges

Police departments have long worked in cooperation with private security forces—to some extent. While private security guards may have little or no law enforcement authority beyond that of any private citizen, they can help a police department by serving as extra "eyes and ears" in certain neighborhoods, downtown areas, or facilities such as shopping centers, entertainment venues, hospitals, educational facilities, businesses, warehouses, critical infrastructure facilities, and other locations.

A number of police chiefs have observed that as they look at the future of their profession, they see that in some ways, public police departments work in *competition* with private security. Especially during an economic downturn—as municipal budgets shrink and police departments lay off officers—neighborhoods and businesses that can afford it increase their use of private security to compensate for reductions in police presence. And because private security guards generally have lower levels of education and training than sworn police officers, they can be hired more cheaply than sworn officers.

Wade Setter, superintendent of the Minnesota Bureau of Criminal Apprehension, described an extreme example of how private security could impact law enforcement. To save money, the small town of Foley, Minnesota, considered *replacing* its law enforcement service with a private security company. However, the town eventually decided to continue using public law enforcement officers after receiving a negative public reaction and opposition from the Minnesota Attorney General and the Minnesota Board of Peace Officer Standards and Training (POST Board).

The director of the POST Board said, "The issue is what a security officer could actually do, because they are not sworn peace officers. A security company employee could not make traffic stops or search a suspect." A letter from Minnesota Attorney General Lori Swanson office warned the city that the use of private security for armed patrol services could cause "considerable statutory and constitutional issues.... Many of these issues could result in financial exposure for the municipality."[23]

> *"Why don't we think outside the box? Why are we worried about private security? Why don't we make them a partner and help train them? I can't police everything in my city. They can help us in reducing crime, and at the end of the day isn't that the issue? I'm not worried about competition. Use private security as a partner to help achieve your goals and make your city safe."*
>
> —Jim Fox, Chief
> Newport News, Virginia, Police Department

---

23. www.docstoc.com/docs/101263450/Letter-from-Minnesota-attorney-general-to-Foley-mayor

There is also an issue of sworn officers supplementing their income by working additional hours during their off-duty time for private entities. Some departments frown on off-duty work at locations such as liquor stores and bars, while other departments see value in those assignments. St. Paul Police Chief Tom Smith recommends that if a department allows employees to "moonlight," it should have strong policies in place to regulate and approve assignments. Smith said that "off-duty employment is one thing that can get chiefs in a lot of trouble. Off-duty officers are wearing our uniform, they're carrying our gear, and so they still need to be bound by the rules and regulations of our organization."

Minneapolis officials emphasized that it is critical to supervise off-duty officers properly and require off-duty officers to maintain communication with on-duty officers in the area. Minneapolis also prohibits its officers from working as bouncers.

To improve communications between the Minneapolis Police Department and private security guards and off-duty officers, the police established a shared radio channel in the downtown area, which Dolan believes has contributed to a virtual elimination of bank robberies in the area. Dolan said, "It's amazing how that partnership has paid off for us."

Other cities, such as Bloomington, Minnesota, have mandated that any contracts for off-duty officers must go through the city. This allows the department to approve or reject assignments, set the terms of any off-duty work, and control the rates charged for off-duty officers. Cherry, who is from Baltimore, said, "We can convince our private-sector partners that they are better off working with professional police officers who know the city, know how to communicate with people in the community, and know how to go to court and get good convictions."

Chief Floyd Simpson of Corpus Christi, however, sees hidden costs in off-duty employment. For example, if an officer is injured while working an off-duty job, the city would have to pay the worker's compensation.

Police Chief Ken Miller of Greensboro, North Carolina, is glad to have private security as a partner in his city. Private security fulfills certain roles that he said "quite frankly we prefer our officers not do, such as building security. It's a better use of our dollars and time. We would be pulling teeth to find officers who would want to do it. So I think there are ways to incorporate private security into the work we do without the fear of them taking over our responsibilities."

# Future Trends in Technology

This chapter summarizes PERF's survey findings and discussions at the Future Trends in Policing Summit regarding technologies that are bringing fundamental changes to policing.

## Police Increasingly Are Using Social Media

Police departments across the country are embracing a variety of social media platforms, and that trend is expected to continue, as **98 percent of PERF survey respondents** said that their agency will increase their use of social media within the next two to five years.

**Table 4:** PERF Survey Questions: What types of social media does your agency currently use? And what types of social media do you plan to begin using within the next 2 to 5 years?

| Social media | % of agencies currently using | % of agencies planning to begin using in 2 to 5 years |
|---|---|---|
| Agency website | 100% | |
| Facebook | 82% | 14% |
| Twitter | 69% | 18% |
| YouTube | 48% | 20% |
| LinkedIn | 34% | 20% |

Police departments are using social media for a variety of reasons for two basic purposes: *disseminating* their own messages to the public, and *gathering* information from social media platforms to prevent and investigate crimes. Many agencies are using social media or expect to do so in the future in order to facilitate criminal investigations (e.g., observing suspects' postings on Facebook for self-incriminating comments), be aware of the mood of the public during major demonstrations, share important information with the public during times of crisis as well as about everyday news and events, receive crime tips, and receive crime reports. A 2013 publication by PERF and the COPS Office, *Social Media and Tactical Considerations for Law Enforcement*,[24] notes that in many larger jurisdictions, the community expects their police department to have a social media presence through platforms such as Twitter, Facebook, and YouTube.

The Los Angeles Police Department (LAPD) has used social media to help guide department operations during major events such as the NBA All Star Game in 2011 and the Stanley Cup playoffs in 2012. During these events, the department tracked large-scale parties and other gatherings throughout the city, and deployed teams of building inspectors, police officers, and fire department officials to ensure the events were legal and safe. The department also monitored social media to keep tabs on "trending" topics, such as whether large crowds of

---

24. Police Executive Research Forum, *Social Media and Tactical Considerations for Law Enforcement* (Washington, DC: Office of Community Oriented Policing Services, 2013), http://ric-zai-inc.com/Publications/cops-p261-pub.pdf.

people planned to head downtown, and adjusted deployment plans accordingly. The LAPD has fully integrated its social media branch into the command post structure for major events, and the social media branch is responsible for briefing the incident commander about relevant activities on social media.

LAPD officers don't just monitor social media, however—they also send out messages of their own. Often, the messages are meant to encourage law-abiding behavior and show good faith on the part of the department in managing major events peacefully. LAPD Deputy Chief Pat Gannon also noted that police messages can sometimes have a subtext of warning for potential lawbreakers. "In some cases, we want people to know how many officers we have deployed. We want to give out information that will give a potential offender pause if they are thinking about causing harm to an event or area," Gannon said.

The Albuquerque Police Department uses free programs, such as Tweet Deck, to stay in touch with the community. A wide variety of Twitter analytics tools are available, many of which are free.[25] Using these real time search tools, departments can stay informed about trending topics in their community. In Albuquerque, officers have been able to anticipate and respond to potential issues by monitoring tweets containing certain keywords. Chief Jeff Tate of Shakopee, Minnesota, described how his officers and their private security partners have monitored social media to intercept rival gangs and, in one instance, even prevented them from causing disruptions at a major amusement park.

Law enforcement agencies must also consider how their own actions are reported to the public through social media. Nearly any public action of a police officer may be recorded on a mobile device and can be instantly uploaded to a social media site. Many of today's police chiefs have said that they generally advise their officers to always behave in public as if they are being recorded, because that very well may be the case.

---

25. IACP's Center for Social Media has useful resources on social media available at www.iacpsocialmedia.org/Technologies/Parent/Platform.aspx?termid=56&depth=3.
Also, Twitter analytics tools are discussed at http://socialmediatoday.com/SMC/192464.

# The Nationwide Public Safety Broadband Network Will Have a Major Impact on Policing

The attacks of 9/11 highlighted serious deficiencies in the ability of police, firefighters, and other first responders to communicate with one another during major multi-jurisdictional responses. The 9/11 Commission Report, which was tasked with analyzing the attacks and the government response to them, said that "the inability to communicate was a critical element at the World Trade Center, Pentagon, and Somerset County, Pennsylvania, crash sites.... The occurrence of this problem at three very different sites is strong evidence that compatible and adequate communications systems among public safety organizations at the local, state, and federal level remains an important problem." The report went on to recommend that Congress "support pending legislation which provides for the expedited and increased assignment of radio spectrum for public safety purposes."[26] For the next decade, public safety officials worked to improve emergency communications, and a major advance took place in 2012.

On February 22, 2012, President Obama signed a bill that includes provisions to fund and govern a Nationwide Public Safety Broadband Network (NPSBN). According to the Department of Homeland Security's Office of Emergency Communications, the NPSBN will "provide a secure, reliable and dedicated interoperable network for emergency responders to communicate during an emergency."[27] The legislation allocated the "D-block" section of

> **THE NATIONWIDE PUBLIC SAFETY BROADBAND NETWORK (NPSBN) WILL HAVE A MAJOR IMPACT ON LAW ENFORCEMENT COMMUNICATIONS IN THE UNITED STATES**
>
> San Jose Chief Chris Moore, who was involved in discussions to establish the NPSBN, encouraged law enforcement leaders to engage with FirstNet, and summarized the importance of reliable wireless broadband capabilities in policing:
>
> "The network will be integral to how policing is done in this country over the next 40–50 years. It's pretty clear that resources for local and state law enforcement have diminished. It's imperative that police become more efficient, and technology will allow this. We have to find ways to leverage this network to help us solve crimes more quickly and efficiently. With this broadband capability, we will be able to securely and reliably use applications that we can't even anticipate yet."
>
> To take one example, Moore said the network could be used to stream video from officers' body-worn cameras. "In the United States, law enforcement agencies pay over $2 billion per year to settle cases of alleged police misconduct. With body-worn cameras, you will eliminate a lot of that. The network can also be used for real time crime centers, to send information to and from the field."

---

26. "The 9/11 Commission Report," page 397. Available online at www.9-11commission.gov/report/911Report.pdf.
27. Office of Emergency Communications, "Nationwide Public Safety Broadband Network," (Washington, DC: U.S. Department of Homeland Security, 2012), www.dhs.gov/sites/default/files/publications/Fact%20Sheet_Nationwide%20Public%20Safety%20Broadband%20Network.pdf.

the radio spectrum to public safety use and provided $7 billion in funding to help construct the network. The bill created an independent authority within the Department of Commerce, called FirstNet, which is responsible for deploying the network. Several law enforcement representatives are part of FirstNet.[28]

> **POTENTIAL BENEFITS OF NG 911**
> - 911 operators will receive better information including text, images, and video data
> - Public safety answering points (PSAP), also known as 911 call centers, will be more flexible, secure, and robust. Increased information sharing will help improve emergency response
> - Users can contact 911 from any networked device
> - PSAPs can more easily transfer emergency calls and back up other PSAPs
>
> *Source: U.S. Department of Transportation Research and Innovative Technology Administration*

## Next Generation 911: Benefits and Challenges

Many public safety agencies are working to establish Next Generation 911 (NG 911) capabilities that will better serve today's wireless society. 911 systems that are capable of receiving text messages, photographs, and videos will be more useful for public safety purposes.

The U.S. Department of Transportation summarized the issue: "Challenges faced by emergency call centers prevent easy transmission of data and critical sharing of information that can significantly enhance the decision-making ability, response, and quality of service provided to emergency callers."[29]

Floyd Simpson, chief of the Corpus Christi Police Department, added that the ability to text 911 is extremely useful for the deaf and hard of hearing community. According to Simpson, updating 911 centers, "isn't just about a new generation of people, it's also about serving a special needs community."

Several recent cases demonstrate the value of texting for emergency assistance. In May 2013, Jimmy Council, the police chief of Kemp, Texas, was assisting on a call for service when he fell 14 feet into an abandoned well that was hidden from view. The bottom of the well

---

28. For a full list of board members see www.commerce.gov/news/fact-sheets/2012/08/20/fact-sheet-first-responder-network-authority-firstnet.
29. "Next Generation 9-1-1: Research Overview," U.S. Department of Transportation, Research and Innovative Technology Administration, www.its.dot.gov/ng911/.

was filled with approximately 8 feet of water. Council attempted to call 911 for assistance, but could not receive adequate service to connect the call. However, he was able to send a text message to the city secretary, who then called 911. The chief was rescued by other law enforcement officials and fire fighters. He credits the text message with saving his life.

In an incident in Black Hawk County, Iowa (the first location in the country to introduce text to 911 service), a woman locked herself in her bedroom when she heard an individual break into her home. She was afraid that making any noise would reveal her location to the intruder, so she texted 911. Law enforcement responded and made an arrest and the woman was unharmed.[31]

The state of Vermont also reported to the FCC that law enforcement in that state was able to save a life as a result of text to 911 capabilities.[32]

While there seems to be a consensus among many law enforcement leaders regarding the need to implement NG 911, leaders also anticipate that it will present new challenges. Leaders are also concerned that text messages lack important contextual clues that help dispatchers ascertain the nature of an emergency. Chief Noble Wray of the Madison, Wisconsin, Police Department said:

> "Text messaging in 911 is inevitable, and we need to start planning for it. But we should also prepare for the inevitable information gap we'll experience with texts. So much of what we rely upon when we're communicating is voice tone and voice inflection."

*"I don't think it's a matter of whether we are interested in going in the direction of texting. Like smart phones, society is going in that direction whether we go with it or not. Members of the public are already demanding that we have the capability to receive emergency information via text."*

–Robert Lehner, Chief
Elk Grove, California, Police Department

*"We must have the capability for people to report crime via text message."*

–Matt Bostrom, Sheriff
Ramsey County, Minnesota

## POLICE IN WASHINGTON, D.C., USE TEXTING TIP LINE

The Metropolitan Police Department of Washington, D.C., provides the public with a means to communicate with officers about routine matters at any time. Each of the city's seven patrol districts maintain a Yahoo group and Listserv. Residents can contact the Listserv

---

30. Frank Heinz and Ben Russell, "Kemp Chief of Police Texts Rescuers After Falling Into Well," NBCDFW.com, May 8, 2013, www.nbcdfw.com/news/weird/Police-Chief-Texts-Rescuers-After-Falling-Into-Well-206438621.html.
31. Thomas Jennings and Judy Flores, "Texting to 9-1-1 in Black Hawk County Consolidated Communications," Technology Talk *The Police Chief* 77 (April 2010): 138, www.policechiefmagazine.org/magazine/index.cfm?fuseaction=display_arch&article_id=2069&issue_id=42010.
32. See FCC Notice of Proposed Rulemaking, released December 13, 2012, www.fcc.gov/document/text-911-further-notice-proposed-rulemaking.

24 hours a day and the watch commander will respond. Assistant Chief Alfred Durham explains that residents "can write to the Listserv at two in the morning, for example, to ask why there is a police presence outside their home, and they will get a response." The district's supervisors are responsible for monitoring and answering the Listserv, which can be accessed via their desktop computer and their department-provided cell phone. Similarly, the Listserv can be used by police supervisors to rapidly inform many residents about something that's going on in their neighborhood. "It's a very valuable tool to send out real time information. The residents appreciate the information, and it helps them to be our eyes and ears," said Durham.

> **D.C. TEXT TIP LINE LEADS TO ARRESTS**
>
> "Our text tip line has helped us many times. Most recently, there was a case where two females were held against their will for prostitution. A text tip came in that explained the situation and provided the location of the victims. We were able to go to the location and make several arrests. In another case, there was an individual selling controlled substances at a homeless shelter, and we were able to make several arrests there."
>
> –Alfred Durham, Assistant Chief
> D.C. Metropolitan Police Department

The D.C. police also use an anonymous text tip line to gather information to help solve homicides. The tip line, established in 2009 as a partnership between the D.C. Metropolitan Police and the FBI's Washington, D.C., Field Office, has resulted in multiple arrests. The department tells residents to "Give 5-0 the 411 with the Text Tip Line: 50411." The text tip line is also advertised by other media outlets.

The number of tips received on the line has grown significantly every year since it was first introduced. In 2012, over 2,000 tips were received. When someone sends in a text tip, it is automatically sent to the D.C. Command Information Center, which is staffed 24 hours a day. From there, the tip is routed to the appropriate unit of the police department. At times, the tip line has received tips about crime occurring outside of D.C., in which case the department has contacted authorities in other jurisdictions.

Durham believes that the Listserv and the text tip line have helped the department obtain more information than it would have otherwise. He explained that, "People communicate using the methods they are comfortable with. Many people today like to e-mail and text, and they can also use these technologies to send photos and other media. It's direct, with no middleman. Ten years ago, we didn't have this ability, and I think the community really appreciates our responsiveness; it speaks volumes to the community and helps us to build trust. Technology has played a huge role in our reductions in crime, but we can never stop and feel comfortable. We always need to be on the cutting edge."

Elk Grove, California, Chief Robert Lehner emphasized the importance of building relationships with the community in new ways. "We need to learn how to relate and build relationships in ways other than face-to-face meetings, because many younger residents prefer other forms of communication," he said.

## Real Time Crime Centers Are Contributing to Crime Fighting

A number of police departments are finding that "real time crime centers"—facilities that gather vast amounts of crime-related data, such as arrest records, mug shots, and warrant information, and provide it rapidly to officers and investigators in the field—can help in crime investigations and protect officer safety.[33] Pioneered in New York City and Houston, real time crime centers are spreading to other cities and will become an increasingly significant part of policing in coming years. The Houston Police Department employs analysts in its real time crime center who monitor social media during major incidents in progress, such as robberies and shootings. When an incident is reported, the analysts immediately begin searching for information on social media, aiming to provide responding officers with relevant information before they arrive at the scene. Satellite imaging and mapping technology enable a real time picture of police resources throughout the city.

Credit: Shutterstock / Balefire

## Cybercrime Represents a Major Emerging Issue for Law Enforcement

Local police departments across the country are grappling with questions about their role in preventing and investigating cybercrime. Federal law enforcement agencies and private-sector organizations already are involved in these efforts, but many local police departments are unsure of what their role should be—in part because of jurisdictional issues. For example, when a victim finds that his or her bank account has been depleted, the bank may be located far from the victim's residence, and the cybercriminal may be on the other side of the world.

A number of points have been raised about the future of cybercrime and the emerging role of local law enforcement agencies in educating the public about protecting themselves, preventing crimes, encouraging victims to report crimes, and investigating crimes when they are committed:

---

33. See Ramon J. Goni, "NYPD Real Time Crime Center," YouTube, September 9, 2009, www.youtube.com/watch?v=FeZ-Px_EvQ4; New York City Global Partners, "Best Practice: Real Time Crime Center: Centralized Crime Data System," www.nyc.gov/html/unccp/gprb/downloads/pdf/NYC_Safety%20and%20Security_RTCC.pdf; and Joseph D'Amico, "Stopping Crime in Real Time," *The Police Chief* 73, no. 9 (September 2006), www.policechiefmagazine.org/magazine/index.cfm?fuseaction=display_arch&article_id=995&issue_id=92006.

- Cybercrime is vastly under-reported, but even the crimes that are reported show this problem is increasing rapidly. For example, a single cybercrime attack against banks in 2013 involved $45 million in losses—which is more than the total losses from all "traditional" bank robberies in 2011.
- Cybercrime includes a set of new types of crime, such as "hacking" bank accounts or sending fraudulent e-mails that trick victims into revealing their bank account numbers and passwords or other financial information. However, it is also useful to think of cybercrime as new ways of using computers or the Internet to facilitate nearly any traditional type of crime.
- Some police chiefs believe that local police agencies generally have been slow to take on the challenge of cybercrime and identify ways in which they can contribute.
- There is a growing recognition that local police will need to get ahead of the curve, because public trust in the police will be damaged if victims receive no help when they call police. When cybercrime victims tell their story to police, they should not get a "blank stare" from officers, chiefs have said. Local police agencies should learn about ways to help victims to the extent possible.
- One way in which every law enforcement agency can contribute is to encourage all cybercrime victims to report the crime to the Internet Crime Complaint Center (IC3), which is the nation's preeminent clearinghouse of data about cybercrime victimizations. IC3 is a partnership between the FBI and the National White Collar Crime Center.[34] By gathering information about cybercrime victimizations, IC3 helps detect trends and provide information for developing counter-strategies.
- All police officers should receive a certain degree of training about cybercrime, so they will be able to respond to victims in an intelligent way and know what questions to ask, and provide helpful information to residents about protecting themselves against scams and cybercriminals. In addition, police departments should have a number of cybercrime experts who have received a much higher level of training.
- Developing cybercrime expertise in a police department can be challenging, in part because private-sector organizations typically can pay far more than police agencies for persons with the necessary knowledge and skills. Some police chiefs recommend looking within your department for officers or civilians who have an interest in computers and technology, and training these people to be police cybercrime analysts and investigators. Training programs are available from the FBI, the Secret Service, and other federal agencies.
- Partnerships are critically important in the field of cybercrime. Task forces with other local, state, and federal law enforcement agencies can lessen the burden on individual police departments. Universities also can be an excellent resource.[35]

---

34. Additional information is available at www.ic3.gov.
35. PERF will be releasing a publication about the role of local police agencies in preventing and investigating cybercrime in 2014.

## Exploring GPS Applications

Many jurisdictions across the country have used GPS devices to track probationers and parolees; these programs typically are developed by courts and probation or parole departments. In Greensboro, North Carolina, under the leadership of Chief Ken Miller, the police department took the lead in developing a GPS solution to help manage repeat offenders.

Miller first implemented GPS technology while he was at the Charlotte-Mecklenburg Police Department. At the time, he believed the courts and probation were not adequately managing repeat offenders. He began thinking about ways to improve the situation and saw a news story that described a program in Oakland, California, that used GPS technology to monitor gun offenders, and thought a similar program could work in his jurisdiction. He modified the idea, focusing on chronic offenders and attempting to change their behavior through the use of curfews and geographic restrictions, which are monitored and reinforced through the electronic monitoring.

Identifying the repeat offenders who are most likely to succeed with such a program is critical to its success, so the project leaders[36] developed a rigorous selection process. The process begins when the police department or a judge nominates individuals for the monitoring program based on their criminal histories and evidence that they are still engaged in criminal activities. The nomination is then submitted for the consideration of a panel consisting of a district court judge, the District Attorney or his or her designee, and a representative of the police department. If the nomination is approved, a police officer from the electronic monitoring unit will attend the offender's initial court appearances. If the presiding judge orders electronic monitoring, he or she can set the parameters of any curfew or territorial restrictions.

> *"For offenders under monitoring, our rate of recidivism is 7 percent, and there's nothing that matches that. Using GPS technology and incorporating it into our records management system is a huge force-multiplier for us. It's driving down property crimes. It helps us better manage the offending population that is invariably going to be back in our community."*
>
> –Ken Miller, Chief
> Greensboro, North Carolina, Police Department

---

36. Project leaders included Chief Miller, Planning Director Paul Paskoff, and Sgt. David Scheppegrell.

For each offender in the program, the police department compares the locations of monitored offenders with the locations of reported crimes on a daily basis to see if there is any overlap. If a match is observed, officers can follow up to see if the offender was involved in the crime. The police department also attempts to prevent offenders from reverting to a criminal lifestyle by connecting the offenders with service providers.

The principal purpose of the program is to deter offenders from committing crimes. To maximize the deterrent effect of the program, officers clearly articulate to offenders how the program works and what penalties they will suffer for noncompliance. The police department also views the program as a cost saving measure. It costs about $4 per day to monitor each offender—significantly less than housing offenders in jail. In both Charlotte and Greensboro, Miller reports that the offenders under monitoring have had an extremely low recidivism rate.

## Using Technology to Help Fill Personnel Gaps

In Camden, New Jersey, a city with extreme financial problems and historically high crime rates, the police department is using a mix of technology to fight crime. A combination of forfeiture money, a grant from the COPS Office, and state grants allowed the department to develop a Real Time Crime Center. The system fuses different camera systems and allows officers to conduct "virtual patrols" of critical areas, including open-air drug markets. Camden Chief Scott Thomson said that the virtual patrols "allow us to get a return from officers who are on light duty." Another component of the Real Time Crime Center is the city's gunshot detection system. If a gunshot is detected, the cameras in the crime center are moved to record either the location the gun shot was detected or avenues of ingress or egress near the shooting location.

"One of the things we found when we installed our gunshot detection system was that about 30 percent of actual gunshots that occurred were never reported because residents had become so desensitized to the sound," Thomson said. "In one instance, the system detected shots, we were able to quickly respond to its precise location, and we arrested one of our top 10 most violent individuals and recovered five handguns."

Camden also uses license plate readers for several purposes. Officers can flag vehicles that have been used in a drug transaction, and if the license plate readers later get a "hit" on that plate, an alert is sent to officers to inform them that the vehicle has been involved in drug activity.

Future Trends in Technology

In San Francisco, Chief Greg Suhr has focused on bringing technology to the department. SFPD's Chief Information Officer, Susan Merritt, said that "despite San Francisco's proximity to Silicon Valley, we realized we were way behind." The police department has established a virtual clearinghouse of crime data called the "Crime Data Warehouse," which is a web-based portal that allows police employees to access 24 different criminal justice information systems. The system is arranged so that officers do not need any special equipment to access the warehouse—just an Internet connection.

"With our Crime Data Warehouse, officers are able to do incident reporting from the field, so they don't have to drive back to the station. Anything they can do at the station, they can do on a laptop computer, police vehicle computer, or on their department-issued smart phone, which all patrol officers will have by year's end," Merritt said. Suhr launched a project in conjunction with the California Department of Justice to deploy smart phones with the California Law Enforcement Telecommunications Systems (CLETS) data access in addition to access to the Crime Data Warehouse. This initiative has enhanced officers' mobility even further. "Officers are now creating incident reports, running suspects, checking mug shots, taking victim statements—all on the streets with the use of the new smart phones," Merritt added.

## TAPPING INTO THE NEW GENERATION OF TECH-SAVVY OFFICERS

Many police chiefs are noticing the technological skills that many young officers bring to their departments. Chief Ray Schultz of Albuquerque said that "this is a generation that understands technology and wants to use it." He provided an example of how a department can harness the technology skills of officers:

*About six months ago I was out on patrol and I stopped to back up one of our officers, who is 23 years old. He was on his smartphone, and I learned that he had written his own application to access criminal records and photographs of inmates booked into the county jail. He had written it himself.*

*We took that application and spread it throughout the organization, and it didn't cost us anything. Another officer is working on an app so we can look on our smartphones and watch the real-time GPS tracking of offenders on probation or parole. We also have an app under development to map restraining orders. And we have automated our crime mapping process, so every day the crime maps are updated automatically.*

# The Organizational Structure of Policing, and the Next Generation of Law Enforcement

## Does the Current Environment Require New Types of Leadership?

Lou Stephens, Special Agent in Charge of the U.S. Secret Service's Minneapolis Field Office, is among the law enforcement officials nationwide who are asking whether the traditional paramilitary structure of law enforcement agencies is conducive to policing in the 21st century:

> *The new people we are hiring are incredibly well educated and well trained. However, they don't thrive under the type of leadership environment that I was brought up in. We are a very hierarchical organization, and our new agents don't always like to deal with layers and layers of management. One of my challenges is to identify how I can engage, motivate and get the most out of them.*
>
> *I try to put in place a structure so there is direct communication on a regular basis between us. I want to empower them and hear their ideas. I want to get their buy-in, so they won't feel frustrated with what they may perceive as a slow and top-heavy decision-making process.*

### PERF SURVEY RESULTS
61% of respondents say that agencies will experiment with organizational structures over the next 2–5 years.

Joshua Ederheimer, Acting Director of the COPS Office, believes that new leadership approaches are needed. Some departments are having difficulty filling their leadership positions because officers aren't interested in advancing to management levels. Ederheimer thinks departments may need to take steps to make their department more attractive to employees.

One way to do this is allowing officers to specialize. "With this new generation, I think there's really going to be an emphasis on allowing people to grow and thrive in a specialty," Ederheimer said. "This is contrary to the traditional generalist policing, but I think it would help meet a need and keep people at police departments."

Assistant Chief Alfred Durham of the Washington, D.C., Metropolitan Police Department agrees that the field of policing needs new thinking about developing leaders. "We have great young women and men within the department doing great things. But we're going to lose 50 percent of our command staff by 2017, and our younger officers aren't interested in being promoted. They would rather remain as an officer, responsible only for themselves, and make money at part-time employment. So we have to figure out how to prepare future leaders for the agency," Durham said.

LAPD Deputy Chief Pat Gannon agreed that promotion to management is not always an officer's goal. "Younger officers see what captains are responsible for, and they think, 'Those guys are nuts. Why would I want to do that?' We need to make it more attractive for people to promote to those ranks, and to do that, we need to understand what makes the younger generation tick."

Professor Charles Wellford of the University of Maryland identified three themes from the conversation about the future of police leadership at PERF's Summit: "Police need to be more transparent, more accountable, and more evidence-based," he said. These changes require a new type of leadership, and "police should embrace these changes; there's no way to fight them," he said.

Not all changes need to be difficult or monumental, Wellford indicated. For example, he said, police departments can take a step toward transparency and accountability simply by posting the names and work contact information of department employees on their agency website.

## Thinking Big to Reduce Crime and Address Gaps in Community Relationships

Mike Davis, Police Chief of Brooklyn Park, Minnesota, urged police leaders to "think big" about how to permanently alter the conditions that lead to crime and disorder:

> *I think that the work we've done over the past 30 years has been good, but some of the things we've done have only resulted in ephemeral changes. Many of our historically challenged neighborhoods are still structurally distressed. In our inner cities—in Camden, Philadelphia, Minneapolis—look at who is being killed. It's young black males—the same people that most often view the police as illegitimate.*
> 
> *Our solvability rates are dependent upon getting information from the community, so we really need to think about what legitimacy means. It's about more than community policing. We need to consider the root causes of the disconnect between the police and the community.*
> 
> *It's time for us to lay out a vision as a profession of how we can bridge the disconnect. I think we're good at tactically developing things, but what we haven't been able to solve is the relational disconnect between the police and the communities that need us the most. If we aren't viewed as legitimate in these communities, we aren't going to be effective.*

Davis believes these concepts can be operationalized. To do so, leaders need to define goals and expectations. For example, performance evaluations should align with the organization's goals. Officers should be given clear direction about what their mission is within their area of responsibility. "We need a laser-like focus on our goal in the community—and that is to change the conditions that contribute to crime and disorder," Davis said.

> **PERF SURVEY RESULTS**
> 95% of agencies agree that communities will place greater expectations on the police to develop trust and maintain legitimacy in their communities.

Davis acknowledged that police cannot directly control many of the variables that contribute to crime and disorder. However, police can get involved in discussions with people who can play a role—elected officials, school officials, public health representatives, and others. "We can pull ourselves up to the table. As a profession, we don't leverage our influence enough," Davis said.

## Considerations for a New Organizational Structure

Bob Lunney, former Police Chief of Edmonton and the Peel Regional Police Department in Canada and author of *Parting Shots: My Passion for Policing,* believes a new architecture is needed for police agency structures. "Police departments have a problem with too many layers of bureaucracy," Lunney said. "Medium to large departments usually have six to eight layers. It's too many levels to control. It's stifling imagination and reducing the capacity of the organization to innovate."

Lunney argues there are four fundamental levels of policing, and departments should be structured to reflect that. The four levels are:

- Workers – officers and investigators
- Supervisors – sergeants and supervisors of investigations
- Managers
- Executives – the chief and assistant or deputy chiefs

Lunney says there are several advantages to a "flatter" organizational structure. First, flatter structures tend to experience fewer communications barriers. Second, they are better at spreading ideas. They also make it easier to establish clear lines of responsibility.

If departments adopt a flatter structure, they will also likely have to revise their compensation structure. In Lunney's view, departments should give higher compensation to employees who are in direct contact with the public and lower compensation to officers working "on the inside."

Madison, Wisconsin, Chief Noble Wray agreed that modern departments may benefit from a flatter structure. In the past, one of the main functions of middle management was information sharing, he said. However, with widespread use of e-mail and cell phones, police organizations may be able to streamline middle management structures because information can be shared more directly by the individuals involved.

There are potential obstacles to creating flatter organizations, however. Departments operating under consent decrees are sometimes required to maintain specific ratios of supervisors to front-line employees.[37] Additionally, agencies may be viewed as inefficient or as "bucking the system"—thereby opening the department to outside criticism—if they deviate from what are considered "industry standard" ratios of supervisors to officers.

## New Roles for Retired Officers

Chief Dean Esserman from New Haven, Connecticut, is finding ways for retired officers to continue contributing to the department. He noted that when officers retire from most departments, it is an abrupt change, and they may no longer see any opportunity to contribute to the department. Esserman is creating a "cold case" unit to tap into retired detectives' expertise. In the unit, retired detectives work part-time assisting current detectives.

Lunney added that the Edmonton Police Department uses retired officers for communications functions. He said this works very well because the retired officers have a depth of experience that is needed for communicating well. According to Elk Grove Chief Bob Lehner, California also has an effective program allowing retirees to contribute to police departments. Retirees can be paid just a part-time salary, with no benefit expenses incurred by the department, and they are allowed to work up to 960 hours per year.

---

37. Police Executive Research Forum, *Civil Rights Investigations of Local Police: Lessons Learned* (Washington, DC: Police Executive Research Forum, July 2013), http://policeforum.org/library/critical-issues-in-policing-series/CivilRightsInvestigationsofLocalPolice.pdf.

## Conclusion: Some of the Details are Unclear, but the Future of Policing Looks Good

It seems undeniable that police departments today are changing more rapidly than at any time in history.

As recently as the 1950s or 1960s, police generally saw their mission as (1) responding to calls for service and (2) investigating crimes. And for most of the 20th century, many years would go by without any significant improvements in the technologies used by local police departments.

Today, police departments are far more complex than they were a generation or two ago. They still respond to calls for service, and they still investigate crimes, but that is where the similarities end. At the most fundamental level, police have expanded their mission, taking on the goal of preventing crime and reducing crime rates, rather than merely responding after crimes are committed. Today's best police departments are always looking for ways to be proactive instead of reactive.

And they have succeeded in this broader mission. Nationwide, violent crime rates are roughly half of what they were in the early 1990s.[38]

Police departments have achieved these goals in large part by deploying an endless array of new strategies and new technologies, such as:

- Community policing
- Problem-oriented policing
- CompStat
- Hot spots policing
- Crime mapping
- Predictive analytics
- Intelligence-led policing
- Closed-circuit video cameras, dash cams, and body cameras
- Automated license plate readers
- Gunshot detection systems
- Wireless transmission of nearly any type of data imaginable
- GPS devices to track suspects
- Sharing of information
- Regional task forces to address gun crime, drug crime, and other issues
- Partnerships with the community, the private sector, and corporations/businesses
- Social media

---

38. www.npr.org/2012/01/03/144627627/falling-crime-rates-challenge-long-held-beliefs

There is no doubt that this overall trend—police agencies expanding their mission and using new strategies and technologies in a proactive way to achieve success—will continue. In fact, the trend almost certainly will accelerate in coming years.

It is difficult to predict the exact outcomes of all these changes, because the field of policing is just beginning to scratch the surface of what is possible. And there are major unknown factors. For example, the vast network of cameras in most cities and towns, combined with advances in facial recognition software and license plate readers, could eventually make it almost impossible for wanted criminals to "hide in plain sight." In fact, there are existing examples of terrorist suspects being quickly identified and apprehended because their images were captured by video cameras. But the courts have not yet weighed in on whether these combinations of technology may be limited in order to avoid violations of constitutionally protected civil liberties or privacy rights. Law enforcement executives may find that police will not be allowed to use every type of technology simply because it is available.

And in some areas, changes are simply too recent to have produced any consensus in policing about best approaches and policies. For example, cybercrime is clearly a growing threat that must be dealt with, and federal law enforcement agencies and private institutions such as banks have been working to get a handle on measures to prevent and investigate these crimes. But with a number of exceptions, most local police departments have not yet found the roles that they will play in fighting cybercrime.

Police executives have just begun to discuss how changes in the new generations of young people will affect how police departments are organized and managed. There seems to be broad agreement that today's young people are bright, ambitious, impatient to achieve things, and less inclined than past generations to stick with a single job, or even a single career, over a lifetime. Some of the wisest police chiefs today are saying they can't expect the younger generation to accept the hierarchical, paramilitary structures of most police departments. Rather, they say, police departments must do the adapting, or they will miss out on hiring and retaining many of the brightest young people.

Today's police leaders also are paying more attention to the question of how they develop the leaders of tomorrow. It's not enough for a chief to reduce crime and develop model policies and practices. Police chiefs increasingly are focusing on building the leadership skills of everyone in the organization, and ensuring that there is a strong bench of second-tier and mid-level leaders. These are the people who help to achieve today's successes, and who must be ready to step up and continue the advances when the current chief retires or moves to a new job.

There is little doubt that police departments and police chiefs will take on and manage all of these new challenges, if for no other reason than that the public will demand it. For 20 years or more, police departments across the country have been recognizing the importance of community policing, public trust, accountability, and transparency in nearly everything they do. Today, these concepts have become ingrained in most police departments; community policing and public trust are part of the DNA of policing.

In the last few years, police chiefs have been discussing the ideas of "legitimacy" and "procedural justice" in policing. These concepts have to do with the judgments that members of the public make about their local police, and whether citizens believe they are being treated fairly and respectfully by the police. Legitimacy and procedural justice sometimes are seen as a new, high-powered version of community policing.

There is no turning back from these principles of public trust, community policing, and legitimacy in policing. Today's police executives understand that they must earn the trust of their community every day.

Thus, to the extent that society is changing and technology is advancing, policing inevitably is advancing as well. Today, the public simply expects that their local police will be in step with what they want from the police. Often, when police executives gather to discuss some new challenge facing police, such as cybercrime, chiefs will say, "We need to get ahead of the curve on this. We don't have any choice. It's happening, and our community members expect us to handle it."

With regard to rapid and sweeping changes in policing, it is perhaps an advantage that the United States has approximately 18,000 separate, autonomous law enforcement agencies nationwide. Such extreme decentralization may have disadvantages in terms of efficiency or cohesion, but in an era of fast change, having 18,000 separate "laboratories" looking for better ways of doing things may produce a greater diversity in approaches. A key challenge for the future may be to ensure that we identify which approaches are working best, and disseminate information about promising practices and policies, so they can be replicated elsewhere. Partnerships with research institutions and private-sector organizations, and advances in technology—such as Next Generation 911 systems—are among the emerging promising practices discussed in this report.

Most experienced police chiefs tell PERF that they enjoy their work and find it complex and fascinating. If we try to imagine what policing will look like a decade from now, the details are blurry in spots, but there is little doubt that the field will continue to grow more complex and interesting for its practitioners.

# Appendixes

## APPENDIX A: Definitions of Policing Strategies

**Community Policing** – a philosophy that promotes organizational strategies, which support the systematic use of partnerships and problem-solving techniques, to proactively address the immediate conditions that give rise to public safety issues such as crime, social disorder, and fear of crime.[39, 40]

**Crime Mapping** – The process of using a geographic information system in combination with crime analysis techniques to focus on the spatial context of criminal and other law enforcement activity.[41]

**Crime Prevention** – The anticipation, recognition, and appraisal of a crime risk and the initiation of some action to remove or reduce it.[42]

**Directed Patrol/Focused Deterrence** – assigning officers to a particular area and freeing them from responding to calls for service so they can engage in proactive investigation and enforcement of suspicious activities.[43]

**Problem-Oriented Policing** – a policing approach that emphasizes the use of analysis and assessment to address crime and disorder problems[44]

**Target Problem Areas/Hot Spots Policing** – identifying and working to reduce crime in small geographical areas in which crime is concentrated.[45]

---

39. http://ric-zai-inc.com/Publications/cops-p157-pub.pdf
40. Daniel W. Flynn, *Defining the "Community" in Community Policing* (Washington, DC: Police Executive Research Forum, July 1998), www.policeforum.org/library/community-policing/cp.pdf.
41. Rachel Boba, *Introductory guide to Crime Analysis and Mapping* (Washington, DC: Office of Community Oriented Policing Services, November 2001), www.cops.usdoj.gov/Publications/introguidecrimeanalysismapping.pdf.
42. National Crime Prevention Council: PPT Presentation located at: http://www.google.com/url?sa=t&rct=j&q=&esrc=s&source=web&cd=1&ved=0CC4QFjAA&url=http%3A%2F%2Fwww.ncpc.org%2Ftraining%2Fpowerpoint-trainings%2Fcrime-prevention-history-and-theory.ppt&ei=rzGiUrvkB8fmsATc0YLgDQ&usg=AFQjCNHPG2usb9N1pcHri0U_XfrWi7oaRA&sig2=ZNoP6RrXScGZrikNMC2Hog&bvm=bv.57752919,d.cWc.
43. Police Executive Research Forum, *Chief Concerns: A Gathering Storm—Violent Crime in America* (Washington, DC: Police Executive Research Forum, October 2006), http://policeforum.org/library/critical-issues-in-policing-series/GatheringStorm-VCinAmerical%28free%29.pdf.
44. "Problem-Oriented Policing," U.S. Department of Justice, Office of Community Oriented Policing Services, www.cops.usdoj.gov/Default.asp?Item=2559.
45. Police Executive Research Forum, *Violent Crime in America: What We Know About Hot Spots Enforcement* (Washington, DC: Police Executive Research Forum, May 2008), http://policeforum.org/library/critical-issues-in-policing-series/HotSpots_v4.pdf.

# APPENDIX B: PERF Survey Results

SURVEY: FUTURE OF POLICING

## Agency Structure and Functions

1. In the next 2 to 5 years, what do you expect to happen for sworn employees? (Select all that apply)

| Action | Increase in the next 2 to 5 years | Decrease in the next 2 to 5 years | Stay the same |
|---|---|---|---|
| Furloughs (N=172) | 7.6% (n=13) | 13.4% (n=23) | 79.1% (n=136) |
| Salary (N=189) | 71.4% (n=135) | 6.3% (n=12) | 22.2% (n=42) |
| Mandated increased employee contributions to pensions (N=188) | 62.2% (n=117) | 4.8% (n=9) | 33.0% (n=62) |
| Layoffs (N=177) | 10.2% (n=18) | 9.6% (n=17) | 80.2% (n=142) |
| Forced retirements (N=175) | 13.1% (n=23) | 11.4% (n=20) | 75.4% (n=132) |

Most agencies predict *increases* in sworn employee salaries (71.4 percent) and mandated increases in employee contributions to pensions (62.2 percent) in the next five years. More than three quarters of respondents predict *no change* in officer furloughs (79.1 percent), layoffs (80.2 percent), and forced retirements (75.4 percent).

2. What changes do you anticipate making in your agency personnel in the next 2 to 5 years? (Select all that apply)

| Personnel | Increase in the next 2 to 5 years | Decrease in the next 2 to 5 years | Stay the same |
|---|---|---|---|
| Number of sworn officers (N=187) | 49.7% (n=93) | 17.6% (n=33) | 32.6% (n=61) |
| Number of civilian employees (N=187) | 42.8% (n=80) | 17.6% (n=33) | 39.6% (n=74) |
| Number of civilian volunteers (N=185) | 67.6% (n=125) | 0.5% (n=1) | 31.9% (n=59) |

Most agencies see the number of sworn and civilian employees as either *staying the same* (32.6 and 39.6 percent), or *increasing* (49.7 and 42.8 percent) in the next five years. Only 17.6 percent of respondents indicated that they anticipate the number of either sworn or civilian employees *decreasing* in the next 2 to 5 years. Over two thirds of respondents (67.6 percent) foresee an *increase* in the number of civilian volunteers in the next 2–5 years—only one agency anticipates the number of volunteers to *decrease*.

3. What changes in delivery of services do you anticipate in the next 2 to 5 years? (Select all that apply)

| Services | Increase in next 2 to 5 years | Decrease in next 2 to 5 years | Do not anticipate change | N responding to frequency question |
|---|---|---|---|---|
| Telephone crime reporting | 60.7% (n=71) | 2.6% (n=3) | 36.8% (n=43) | N=117 |
| Online crime reporting | 82.1% (n=119) | 0 | 17.9% (n=26) | N=145 |
| 911 dispatchers send/receive texts | 74.4% (n=122) | 0 | 25.6% (n=42) | N=164 |
| Reverse 911 | 60.0% (n=66) | 0.9% (n=1) | 39.1% (n=43) | N=110 |
| Officers respond to calls for service via telephone | 41.4% (n=60) | 2.1% (n=3) | 56.6% (n=82) | N=145 |
| Crime victims can check case status online | 59.0% (n=102) | 0 | 41.0% (n=71) | N=173 |
| Follow up calls to crime victims | 54.8% (n=69) | 9.5% (n=12) | 35.7% (n=45) | N=126 |
| Follow up calls to those who report crime | 39.9% (n=55) | 10.1% (n=14) | 50.0% (n=69) | N=138 |
| Non-sworn response to certain calls for service | 56.6% (n=82) | 1.4% (n=2) | 42.1% (n=61) | N=145 |

The majority of respondents (82.1 percent) anticipate an *increase* in the use of online crime reporting in the next 2 to 5 years. Other trends that many foresee *increasing* are: 911 dispatchers sending/receiving text messages (74.4 percent), telephone crime reporting (60.7 percent), reverse 911 (60.0 percent), case status check online for victims (59.0 percent), and non-sworn response to certain calls for service (56.6 percent). Very few agencies predict that any of the listed service delivery methods will *decrease* in the next 2 to 5 years. However, 56.6 percent do not anticipate a change in officers responding to calls for service via telephone, and 50.0 percent believe follow-up calls to those who report crime will not change.

4. What are the minimum education requirements for incoming recruits?

| Education | 5 years ago (N=137) | Current (N=184) | Expected in 5 years (N=153) |
|---|---|---|---|
| High school | 66.4% (n=91) | 69.0% (n=127) | 38.6% (n=59) |
| Some college | 13.1% (n=18) | 10.3% (n=19) | 26.1% (n=40) |
| 2-year degree | 16.8% (n=23) | 16.8% (n=31) | 24.2% (n=37) |
| 4-year degree | 3.6% (n=5) | 3.8% (n=7) | 11.1% (n=17) |

About two thirds of responding agencies required a minimum of a high school diploma five years ago (66.4 percent) and currently (69.0 percent). However, only 38.6 percent of agencies believe that will be the case in five years—50.3 percent of respondents anticipate requiring either some college or a two year degree and 11 percent requiring a four year degree.

## CRIME TRENDS AND CRIME FIGHTING STRATEGIES

5. What three crimes or issues do you think will have the greatest impact on public safety in your community in the next 2 to 5 years (e.g., burglary, robbery, or aggravated assault)? (Fill in blanks below)

| Violent crime | 251 |
|---|---|
| Robbery | 92 |
| Aggravated assault | 70 |
| Homicide | 20 |
| Gang crime | 19 |
| Domestic violence | 16 |
| Gun crime | 15 |
| General violent crime | 11 |
| Sexual assault | 8 |

| Property crime | 215 |
|---|---|
| Burglary | 119 |
| Theft | 26 |
| Larceny | 23 |
| General property crime | 20 |
| Financial crime/fraud | 17 |
| Auto theft | 10 |

| Other crime | 96 |
|---|---|
| Drug crime | 37 |
| Other crime* | 32 |
| Internet/cybercrime | 19 |
| Impaired driving | 8 |

*Examples of responses classified as "Other Crime" include prostitution, traffic offenses, human smuggling, crime against elders, parolee crime, and mental illness.

Respondents identified burglary (n=119), robbery (n=92), and [non-sexual/firearm] aggravated assault (n=70) as the three crimes having the greatest impact on public safety in their community. Responses were split rather evenly between violent crimes (n=251) and property crimes (n=215). Drug crime (n=37) was also a common response.

6. What strategies do you expect your agency to use in the next 2 to 5 years? (Please mark all that apply)

| Strategy | Currently use | Implement or increase in next 2 to 5 years | Eliminate or decrease in next 2 to 5 years |
|---|---|---|---|
| Community policing | 93.7% | 31.7% | 2.6% |
| CompStat | 66.1% | 30.2% | 7.9% |
| Problem-oriented policing | 88.9% | 34.9% | 1.6% |
| Hot Spot Policing | 79.9% | 41.3% | 2.6% |
| Directed police patrols / focused deterrence | 92.1% | 35.4% | 2.1% |
| Targeting known offenders | 79.3% | 47.3% | 2.1% |
| Targeting specific problem addresses/locations | 91.5% | 39.2% | 1.1% |
| Information/intelligence-led policing | 72.7% | 54.0% | 1.6% |
| Predictive policing | 38.2% | 70.4% | 2.2% |
| Crime prevention programs | 90.5% | 29.6% | 4.2% |
| Violence prevention programs | 69.5% | 37.4% | 3.2% |
| Real time crime center | 18.0% | 54.6% | 6.0% |
| Regional fusion center | 65.6% | 36.0% | 2.7% |
| Intelligence databases | 76.5% | 44.4% | 0.0% |
| Crime mapping | 86.2% | 40.4% | 0.0% |
| Crime analysis | 85.1% | 45.7% | 0.0% |
| Regional task forces | 80.4% | 31.7% | 5.3% |

Most respondents indicated that they *currently use* community policing (93.7 percent), directed patrol/focused deterrence (92.1 percent), target problem addresses/locations (91.5 percent), crime prevention programs (90.5 percent), problem-oriented policing (88.9 percent), crime mapping (86.2 percent), crime analysis (85.1 percent), and regional task forces (80.4 percent). Many agencies anticipate *implementing* predictive policing (70.4 percent) strategies in the next 2 to 5 years (currently only 38.2 percent use this strategy). Additionally, 54.0 percent of respondents anticipate *implementing or increasing* their use of information or intelligence-led policing. There are no particular strategies that **many** agencies intend on *eliminating or decreasing*.

Appendixes

## REGIONALIZATION, CONSOLIDATION, AND PRIVATIZATION

7. What regionalization, consolidation, or privatization measures will your agency consider in the future? (Select all that apply)

| Measures | Currently doing | Next 2 to 5 years | Not currently doing and no immediate plans to start |
|---|---|---|---|
| Consolidating district stations w/in agency | 9.6% | 7.0% | 84.0% |
| Consolidating units w/in agency | 35.6% | 17.6% | 52.1% |
| Eliminating some specialized units | 22.6% | 20.7% | 59.0% |
| Merging some specialized functions (e.g., swat, aviation, or marine) with other local police departments to create regional units | 27.1% | 23.4% | 54.3% |
| Outsourcing police services or functions to private vendors (e.g., forensic lab) | 21.8% | 19.7% | 61.7% |
| Privatizing some police services (e.g., replace with private security) | 9.0% | 16.5% | 75.0% |
| Merging with one or more other local police departments | 4.8% | 9.0% | 87.2% |
| Merging with fire department(s) to create combined public safety agency | 6.3% | 3.7% | 89.4% |
| MOU to use another local agency's specialized function (e.g., SWAT, aviation, or forensic lab) | 42.3% | 18.0% | 42.3% |
| MOU to provide some of our specialized functions to other local agencies | 50.3% | 24.3% | 30.7% |

Most responding agencies have no current or future regionalization, consolidation, or privatization plans—however, some agencies are sharing or planning to share specialized resources. The only areas where a noteworthy number of respondents are merging forces are in providing some specialized functions to other local agencies (50.3 percent), and using another local agencies' specialized functions (42.3 percent). Just under one quarter of respondents anticipate merging some specialized functions (23.4 percent) or providing specialized functions to other local agencies (24.3 percent) in the next 2 to 5 years.

8. In the wake of the current economic crisis, please describe any innovative ways your agency is providing public safety through the regionalization, consolidation, and/or privatization of policing services. If you don't have any examples to provide, please mark N/A in the space provided.

As indicated in question seven, some agencies are sharing resources with other local agencies. The most common type of regionalized task forces are: 911/Dispatch services (n=24) and SWAT (n=18). However, it must be noted that given the wording of the question these numbers do not necessarily represent what agencies are doing, just what they are doing *and* perceive to be innovative.

| Regionalization, consolidations, and privatization initiatives | Type of cost-saving resource/function | # of LE agencies participating | Specific examples |
|---|---|---|---|
| Regional teams, units, and task forces | Regional 911/dispatch | 24 | |
| | Regional SWAT | 18 | |
| | Regional task force (general) | 10 | |
| | Regional drug team | 9 | |
| | Regional training | 8 | |
| | Regional RMS | 7 | |
| | Regional analysis/intel | 6 | |
| | Regional/state forensics | 6 | |
| | Regional gang unit | 5 | |
| | Regional air unit | 5 | |
| | Regional auto theft unit | 4 | |
| | Regional bomb team | 4 | |
| | Regional K-9 unit | 4 | |
| | Regional child crime unit | 4 | |
| | Regional negotiators | 3 | |
| | Regional detention centers | 3 | |
| | Regional dive team | 3 | |
| | Regional cybercrime | 3 | |
| | Regional drunk/DUI unit | 2 | |
| | Regional CIT | 2 | |
| | Regional task force (other) | 21 | (Administrative services, fraud task force, medical strike team, victim liaison, hazmat, crowd control, sex predator, domestic violence, traffic, emergency management, motor unit, theft unit) |
| Shared resources | Shared technology | 3 | |
| | Shared building | 3 | |
| Citizen involvement | Volunteers/interns | 11 | |
| | Civilians | 3 | |
| Private sector partnership | Private security guards | 5 | |
| | Private sector partnerships (general) | 3 | |
| | Private sector partnerships (other) | 3 | (False alarm program, impound, internal affairs) |
| | Private jail | 2 | |
| | Private victim services | 2 | |
| | Private forensics | 2 | |
| Other | Federal partnership (JTTF) | 6 | |
| | Other | 3 | (Contract with military, consolidate administrative staff, share grant coordinator) |

Appendixes

## PARTNERSHIPS

9. What partnerships with non law enforcement agencies does your agency currently use or expect to use in the future? (Select all that apply)

| Partnership | Currently doing | Next 2 to 5 years | Not currently doing and no immediate plans to start |
|---|---|---|---|
| Businesses/corporations | 69.3% | 21.2% | 14.8% |
| Non-profit or NGO | 79.9% | 15.9% | 10.6% |
| Police foundations | 45.5% | 22.8% | 35.4% |
| Private security companies | 33.9% | 12.2% | 54.5% |
| Other local law enforcement agencies | 93.7% | 11.1% | 2.6% |
| Other private organizations | 54.0% | 13.2% | 28.0% |

Nearly all of responding agencies are currently partnering with other local law enforcement agencies (93.7 percent), and a vast majority is currently working with non-profits or NGOs (79.9 percent), and businesses or corporations (69.3 percent). While one third of respondents are currently partnering with private security companies (33.9 percent), over half (54.5 percent) have no plans to do so.

10. If you are currently using or planning to use non law enforcement partnerships, please describe. If you don't have any examples to provide, please mark N/A in the space provided.

| Partnership | n | Examples |
|---|---|---|
| Non-profit organizations | 53 | Rotary Club, Lions, victims awareness, MADD, YWCA, United Way, child advocacy centers, senior centers |
| Schools/universities | 18 | DARE, university police |
| Law enforcement foundations | 12 | Police Foundation, IACP |
| Government agencies | 20 | Department of corrections, department of health |
| Private sector | 40 | Motorola, Target, NASCAR, Lowes, Walmart, Home Depot |
| Religious groups | 11 | Clergy groups, churches |
| Neighborhood association | 9 | Neighborhood associations, apartment complexes |
| Business/commerce organizations | 14 | Chamber of commerce, business associations |

When asked to provide examples, 53 respondents named non-profit organizations, such as Rotary Clubs, Lions, Victims Awareness, MADD, YWCA, United Way, Child Advocacy Centers, and Senior Centers. Forty agencies listed private sector partners, which included major corporations (Motorola, Target, NASCAR, Lowes, Walmart, and Home Depot) as well as local businesses. Some agencies noted that they do not necessarily partner with businesses directly, but work with their local chamber of commerce or other business association (n=14). Note that these are not mutually exclusive categories, as some agencies listed multiple partners.

11. What funding sources, outside of your local budget, does your agency plan to seek in the next 2 to 5 years, and for what purposes will it be used? (Select all that apply)

| Money used to fund... | Federal grants | State grants | Private corporations | Private foundations | Other |
|---|---|---|---|---|---|
| Sworn employees | 79.1% | 47.1% | 3.2% | 5.3% | 4.3% |
| Civilian employees | 50.3% | 60.4% | 4.3% | 5.9% | 5.3% |
| Crime fighting initiative | 74.3% | 63.1% | 20.3% | 25.7% | 2.7% |
| Volunteer programs | 23.1% | 19.9% | 25.3% | 25.8% | 9.1% |
| Technology | 85.7% | 71.4% | 27.0% | 26.5% | 3.2% |
| Equipment | 85.7% | 73.5% | 29.1% | 30.7% | 3.7% |
| Vehicles | 51.1% | 40.9% | 11.3% | 13.4% | 7.5% |

Outside their local budget, respondents anticipate utilizing federal grants to purchase equipment (85.7 percent), technology (85.7 percent), pay sworn salaries (79.1 percent), and fund crime fighting initiatives (74.3 percent) in the next 2 to 5 years. Additionally, respondents anticipate they will use state grants to fund equipment (73.5 percent) and technology (71.4 percent) purchases in the next 2 to 5 years. Less than one third of respondents anticipate funding salaries, programs, or purchases through private corporations or foundations in the next 2 to 5 years.

12. Which of the following does your agency use in partnership with private businesses and/or corporations? (Select all that apply)

| Services | Currently doing | Next 2 to 5 years | Not currently doing and no immediate plans to start |
|---|---|---|---|
| Shared information through database/computer network | 39.7% | 13.2% | 50.8% |
| Interactive partnership website | 26.5% | 19.0% | 57.7% |
| Regular meetings of partnership members | 68.3% | 16.4% | 20.6% |
| Shared radio channel(s) allowing partners to directly communicate with police | 28.6% | 10.1% | 61.4% |
| Cell phones provided to partners for direct communication with police | 14.3% | 10.6% | 75.7% |
| Real-time crime centers | 14.8% | 28.0% | 56.1% |
| Interactive crime mapping | 50.8% | 24.3% | 29.6% |
| Texting of crime tips | 43.4% | 41.8% | 19.6% |
| Shared CCTV cameras | 34.9% | 35.4% | 36.5% |
| License plate readers installed in private parking lots | 12.7% | 36.0% | 50.3% |
| Shared office space or facilities | 42.9% | 20.1% | 40.2% |
| Joint training with private security | 24.3% | 16.4% | 61.9% |
| Training for police officers provided by private corporation | 34.9% | 15.3% | 50.3% |
| Private partners attend court proceedings to show importance of crime-fighting measures | 12.7% | 12.7% | 75.7% |

Agencies appear to be split with regard to partnering with private businesses for various services. The most common current partnerships are meetings with partnership members (68.3 percent), interactive crime mapping (50.8 percent), texting crime tips (43.4 percent), and sharing office space or facilities (42.9 percent). In the next 2 to 5 years, more than a third of respondents plan to work with partners on texting crime tips (41.8 percent), installing license plate readers in private parking lots (36.0 percent), and sharing CCTV cameras (35.4 percent). The majority of responding agencies have no plans to work with partners on court watches (75.7 percent), provide cell phones to partners for direct communication (75.7 percent), have joint training with private security (61.9 percent), or share radio channels with partners (61.4 percent). Many of the choices add up to more than 100 percent because some agencies selected "currently" and "next 2 to 5 years."

## TECHNOLOGY

13. In most areas, there are currently many camera systems in place. Does your agency have access to monitor in real time any of these systems or does it plan to gain access in the next 2 to 5 years to these camera systems? (Mark all that apply)

| Camera system | Currently have real time access | Current access by special request only | Next 2 to 5 years | N/A |
|---|---|---|---|---|
| Traffic | 52.9% | 19.6% | 13.2% | 14.3% |
| Bus | 10.9% | 33.9% | 13.1% | 42.1% |
| Rail | 8.7% | 25.0% | 12.0% | 54.3% |
| Toll booths | 1.1% | 11.0% | 2.7% | 85.2% |
| Public works | 18.4% | 24.3% | 13.0% | 44.9% |
| Housing authorities | 10.4% | 24.0% | 12.6% | 54.1% |
| Schools | 22.9% | 39.4% | 14.9% | 23.4% |
| Private business districts | 18.4% | 25.4% | 21.1% | 36.2% |
| Private businesses | 8.5% | 38.1% | 20.6% | 32.3% |
| Private security | 6.6% | 31.3% | 17.0% | 45.6% |

Responding agencies indicated that they do not have real time access to many camera systems. The most common current real time camera access agencies have is to traffic cameras (52.9 percent). Some agencies can request special access to cameras at schools (39.4 percent), private businesses (38.1 percent), busses (33.9 percent), and private security (31.3 percent), among others.

14. Which social media applications does your agency currently use? (Select all that apply)

| Media | Currently using | Next 2 to 5 years | Not currently using and no immediate plans to start |
|---|---|---|---|
| Facebook | 81.5% | 13.8% | 4.2% |
| Twitter | 69.3% | 17.5% | 12.7% |
| YouTube | 48.1% | 20.1% | 29.6% |
| LinkedIn | 33.9% | 19.6% | 41.8% |
| Agency website | 100.0% | | |

All responding agencies currently utilize a department website. Additionally, most also currently use Facebook (81.5 percent), and Twitter (69.3 percent) for social media, or plan to implement them in the next 2 to 5 years (13.8 percent and 17.5 percent, respectively). Nearly half of respondents (48.1 percent) use YouTube, and 20.1 percent plan to begin using it in the next 2 to 5 years. About half of respondents either currently use (33.9 percent) or plan to use (19.6 percent) LinkedIn for social networking.

15. Does your agency currently use or plan to use in the next 5 years social media applications for any of the following? (Select all that apply)

| Efforts | Currently using | Next 2 to 5 years | Not currently using and no immediate plans to start |
|---|---|---|---|
| Communication to public | 92.1% | 6.9% | 1.1% |
| Crime reporting by public | 55.6% | 23.8% | 20.1% |
| Tips from public | 73.0% | 23.8% | 3.2% |
| Dissemination of press releases | 88.9% | 7.9% | 2.6% |
| Recruiting | 76.2% | 18.0% | 5.8% |
| Monitor large events/demonstrations | 61.4% | 21.2% | 16.9% |
| Monitor general public mood | 50.8% | 25.4% | 22.2% |
| Monitor what is being said about your agency | 69.3% | 18.5% | 11.6% |
| General investigations | 76.2% | 15.9% | 8.5% |
| Undercover investigations | 48.4% | 25.8% | 25.8% |

Currently, most agencies are using social media to communicate to the public (92.1 percent), disseminate press releases (88.9 percent), conduct general investigations (76.2 percent), recruit (76.2), and gather tips from the public (73.0 percent). Many of the agencies that are not currently using social media for the provided reasons plan to do so in the next 2 to 5 years.

16. What efforts does your agency use and expect to use in the next 2 to 5 years to fight cybercrime? (Select all that apply)

| Efforts | Current | Next 2 to 5 years | N/A |
|---|---|---|---|
| Cybercrime investigations by officers/detectives | 77.2% | 11.1% | 11.6% |
| Cybercrime investigations by undercover officers/detectives | 74.5% | 13.8% | 11.7% |
| Specialized unit for cybercrimes | 47.6% | 24.6% | 27.8% |
| Specialized unit for social media investigations | 24.6% | 31.1% | 44.3% |
| Training officers on social media communications | 59.9% | 31.6% | 8.6% |
| Training officers on social media investigations | 57.5% | 33.9% | 8.6% |
| Training officers on computer forensics | 74.2% | 15.6% | 10.2% |
| Collaboration with federal agencies | 93.1% | 3.7% | 3.2% |
| Build relationship with private social media and Internet providers | 45.6% | 38.5% | 15.9% |

Currently, most responding agencies are fighting cybercrime by collaborating with federal agencies (93.1 percent), using officers/detectives (77.2 percent), using undercover officers or detectives (74.5 percent), and training officers on computer forensics (74.2 percent). Few agencies (24.6 percent) currently have specialized units for social media investigations, and many (44.3 percent) have no plans to implement one.

17. Please describe any innovative ways in which your agency has incorporated technology into your overall crime fighting strategy in the space provided.

| Technology | n | % |
| --- | --- | --- |
| Social media / outreach | 31 | 26.3 |
| Cameras / CCTV | 30 | 25.4 |
| Mapping / hot spots / GPS | 25 | 21.2 |
| License plate readers | 22 | 18.6 |
| RMS / shared database / intranet | 20 | 16.9 |
| In-car computer / tablet | 19 | 16.1 |
| Analysis | 14 | 11.9 |
| Computer forensics | 10 | 8.5 |
| In-car camera | 8 | 6.8 |
| Automated / e-ticket device | 8 | 6.8 |
| Online crime reporting | 7 | 5.9 |
| ShotSpotter | 6 | 5.1 |
| CompStat | 6 | 5.1 |
| Cell phone tracking | 6 | 5.1 |
| Text-a-Tip | 5 | 4.2 |
| Inter-agency data sharing | 3 | 2.5 |
| Mobile/electronic fingerprinting | 3 | 2.5 |
| Ballistics partnership | 2 | 1.7 |
| Patrol vehicle locator | 2 | 1.7 |
| Other | 33 | 28.0 |

When asked to describe innovative strategies for incorporating technology into crime fighting strategies, the most common responses were through social media, cameras and CCTV, mapping and hot spots, and license plate readers. These numbers do not necessarily represent what agencies are doing, just what they are doing and perceive to be innovative (for example, it is likely that more than six use CompStat, and more than two track patrol vehicles). Other examples of technology used included digital recording equipment, breathalyzers, Tasers, biometrics, jail phone taps, paperless report writing, Skype conferencing, and monitoring school websites. Totals are out of the 118 agencies that provided an answer to this question. Percentages do not add up to 100, as some agencies listed multiple things.

## FUTURE EXPECTATIONS

For each of the following statements about how policing could change in the next 2 to 5 years please rate the following statements from 1 to 5. (1=Strongly Disagree, 2=Disagree, 3=No Opinion, 4=Agree, 5=Strongly Agree)

### Police Functions and Department Structure

18. Local agencies will focus more resources on data collection, crime analysis, and real-time intelligence.

| Strongly disagree | Disagree | No opinion | Agree | Strongly agree |
|---|---|---|---|---|
| 0.5% | 0.5% | 3.7% | 35.1% | 60.1% |

Nearly all agencies (95.2 percent) agree or strongly agree that local agencies will focus more resources on data collection, crime analysis, and real-time intelligence.

19. Agencies will place less emphasis on community policing.

| Strongly disagree | Disagree | No opinion | Agree | Strongly agree |
|---|---|---|---|---|
| 39.0% | 36.9% | 9.6% | 11.8% | 2.7% |

Three quarters of agencies (75.9 percent) disagree or strongly disagree with the idea that agencies will place less emphasis on community policing.

20. Agencies will direct more resources toward identifying undocumented immigrants and enforcing immigration laws.

| Strongly disagree | Disagree | No opinion | Agree | Strongly agree |
|---|---|---|---|---|
| 23.9% | 42.6% | 22.3% | 9.0% | 2.1% |

Two thirds of agencies (66.5 percent) disagree or strongly disagree with the idea that agencies will direct more resources toward identifying undocumented immigrants and enforcing immigration laws.

21. Local agencies will increase coordination of crime fighting strategies.

| Strongly disagree | Disagree | No opinion | Agree | Strongly agree |
|---|---|---|---|---|
| 0% | 1.6% | 3.7% | 60.8% | 33.9% |

Nearly all agencies (94.7 percent) agree or strongly agree with the statement that local agencies will increase coordination of crime fighting strategies.

22. Police and fire services will be consolidated.

| Strongly disagree | Disagree | No opinion | Agree | Strongly agree |
|---|---|---|---|---|
| 29.8% | 41.0% | 16.0% | 10.1% | 3.2% |

Many respondents (70.8 percent) disagree or strongly disagree with the idea that police and fire services will be consolidated.

## Communication and Influence

23. Agencies will spend more resources building and maintaining their public image or brand.

| Strongly disagree | Disagree | No opinion | Agree | Strongly agree |
|---|---|---|---|---|
| 1.1% | 4.8% | 12.2% | 56.6% | 25.4% |

Many agencies (82.0 percent) agree or strongly agree that agencies will spend more resources building and maintaining their public image or brand.

24. Communities will place greater expectations on the police to develop trust and maintain legitimacy in their communities.

| Strongly disagree | Disagree | No opinion | Agree | Strongly agree |
|---|---|---|---|---|
| 0% | 1.1% | 4.2% | 53.4% | 41.3% |

Nearly all respondents (94.7 percent) either agree or strongly agree that communities will place greater expectations on the police to develop trust and maintain legitimacy in their communities.

25. Agencies will increase their use of social media.

| Strongly disagree | Disagree | No opinion | Agree | Strongly agree |
|---|---|---|---|---|
| 0% | 0.5% | 0.5% | 34.9% | 64.0% |

Nearly all respondents (98.9 percent) either agree or strongly agree that agencies will increase their use of social media.

26. Community members and local businesses will seek greater cooperation with police agencies.

| Strongly disagree | Disagree | No opinion | Agree | Strongly agree |
|---|---|---|---|---|
| 0% | | 5.8% | 63.0% | 31.2% |

Nearly all respondents (94.2 percent) either agree or strongly agree that community members and local businesses will seek greater cooperation with police agencies.

27. Demands by special interest groups will significantly influence police service demands.

| Strongly disagree | Disagree | No opinion | Agree | Strongly agree |
|---|---|---|---|---|
| 1.1% | 14.3% | 34.4% | 41.8% | 8.5% |

Many agencies (50.3 percent) agree or strongly agree that demands by special interest groups will significantly influence police service demands. Interestingly, more than one third of respondents (34.4 percent) indicated that they have no opinion on the topic.

28. Local or state government decision makers will demand greater use of performance measurement of policing activities.

| Strongly disagree | Disagree | No opinion | Agree | Strongly agree |
|---|---|---|---|---|
| 0% | 4.8% | 12.3% | 58.3% | 24.6% |

Many agencies (82.9 percent) agree or strongly agree that local or state government decision makers will demand greater use of performance measurement of policing activities.

## Personnel

29. Agencies will continue to face budget cuts and force reductions.

| Strongly disagree | Disagree | No opinion | Agree | Strongly agree |
|---|---|---|---|---|
| 0% | 11.1% | 10.6% | 57.1% | 21.2% |

Most respondents (78.3 percent) agree or strongly agree that agencies will continue to face budget cuts and force reductions.

30. Agencies will lower their qualifications for new recruits.

| Strongly disagree | Disagree | No opinion | Agree | Strongly agree |
|---|---|---|---|---|
| 27.5% | 49.2% | 11.1% | 9.5% | 2.6% |

Most agencies (76.7 percent) disagree or strongly disagree with the notion that agencies will lower their qualifications for new recruits.

31. It will be more difficult for agencies to hire and retain high-caliber personnel.

| Strongly disagree | Disagree | No opinion | Agree | Strongly agree |
|---|---|---|---|---|
| 5.8% | 28.0% | 14.8% | 40.2% | 11.1% |

There is no clear trend among agencies with regard to future difficultly for agencies hiring and retaining high-caliber personnel. 51.3 percent agree or strongly agree, while 33.8 percent disagree or strongly disagree.

32. Most recruitment efforts will be moved online through social media and the Internet.

| Strongly disagree | Disagree | No opinion | Agree | Strongly agree |
|---|---|---|---|---|
| 0% | 9.6% | 14.9% | 59.6% | 16.0% |

Most agencies agree or strongly agree (75.6 percent) that most recruitment efforts will be moved online through social media and the Internet.

33. Agencies will increasingly use civilians or citizen volunteers to do jobs currently performed by sworn personnel.

| Strongly disagree | Disagree | No opinion | Agree | Strongly agree |
|---|---|---|---|---|
| 4.8% | 20.7% | 16.0% | 48.4% | 10.1% |

Many respondents (58.5 percent) agree or strongly agree that agencies will increasingly use civilians or citizen volunteers to do jobs currently performed by sworn personnel, but 25.5 percent disagree or strongly disagree.

34. Agencies will experiment with traditional command and control organizational structures.

| Strongly disagree | Disagree | No opinion | Agree | Strongly agree |
|---|---|---|---|---|
| 1.1% | 10.1% | 27.5% | 55.6% | 5.8% |

Many agencies (61.4 percent) agree or strongly agree that agencies will experiment with traditional command and control organizational structures, while more than one quarter of respondents (27.5 percent) indicated that they have no opinion.

## Technology

35. Officers will demand a higher level of sophistication in the agency's technological capabilities.

| Strongly disagree | Disagree | No opinion | Agree | Strongly agree |
|---|---|---|---|---|
| 0% | 0.5% | 1.1% | 48.1% | 50.3% |

Nearly all respondents (98.4 percent) agree or strongly agree that officers will demand a higher level of sophistication in the agency's technological capabilities.

36. General technological advances may create unrealistic expectations in the community regarding police agencies' abilities to prevent and solve crimes.

| Strongly disagree | Disagree | No opinion | Agree | Strongly agree |
|---|---|---|---|---|
| 0% | 8.5% | 9.0% | 49.2% | 33.3% |

Most respondents (82.5 percent) agree or strongly agree that general technological advances may create unrealistic expectations in the community regarding police agencies' abilities to prevent and solve crimes.

# APPENDIX C: "Future of Policing" Executive Session Attendees

| Title | First | Last | Agency/organization |
|---|---|---|---|
| Lieutenant | Shon | Barnes | Greensboro (NC) Police Department |
| Sheriff | Matt | Bostrom | Ramsey County (MN) Sheriff's Office |
| President, FOP | Bob | Cherry | Baltimore City FOP Lodge 3 |
| Research Associate | Megan | Collins | Police Executive Research Forum (PERF) |
| Lieutenant | Joel | Cranford | Greensboro (NC) Police Department |
| Chief | Michael | Davis | Brooklyn Park (MN) Police Department |
| Executive Director | Pam | Delaney | National Police Foundations Project |
| Chief | Kim | Dine | Frederick (MD) Police Department |
| Chief | Tim | Dolan | Minneapolis Police Department |
| Assistant Chief | Alfred | Durham | Metropolitan DC Police Department |
| Principal Deputy Director | Joshua | Ederheimer | Office of Community Oriented Policing Services (COPS Office) |
| Ms. | Mahogany | Eller | Target Corporation, Inc. (National Public Safety Strategic Partnerships, Corporate Security) |
| Chief | Dean | Esserman | New Haven (CT) Police Department |
| Chief | James | Fox | Newport News (VA) Police Department |
| Deputy Chief | Patrick | Gannon | Los Angeles Police Department |
| Chief Information Officer | Susan | Giffin | San Francisco Police Department |
| Chief | Ralph | Godbee | Detroit Police Department |
| Legislative Specialist | Kevin | Greene | Police Executive Research Forum (PERF) |
| Assistant Chief | Janeè | Harteau | Minneapolis Police Department |
| Chief | Kim | Jacobs | Columbus (OH) Police Department |
| Chief | Robert | Lehner | Elk Grove (CA) Police Department |
| United States Marshal | Sharon | Lubinski | U.S. Marshals Service |
| Mr. | Andy | Luger | Greene Espel P.L.L.P. |
| Consultant, Police and Public Safety | Robert | Lunney | Robert Lunney Associates |
| Captain | Sean | Malinowski | Los Angeles Police Department |
| Senior Supervisory Policy Analyst | Katherine | McQuay | Office of Community Oriented Policing Services (COPS Office) |
| Policy Analyst | Zoe | Mentel | Office of Community Oriented Policing Services (COPS Office) |
| Chief | Ken | Miller | Greensboro (NC) Police Department |
| Chief | Ron | Miller | Topeka (KS) Police Department |
| Chief | Chris | Moore | San Jose (CA) Police Department |
| Assistant Special Agent in Charge | Daniel | Moren | Drug Enforcement Agency (Minneapolis-St. Paul) |
| Executive Assistant Chief | Kirk | Munden | Houston Police Department |
| Interim Chief | Rick | Myers | Sanford (FL) Police Department |
| Senior Administrative Manager | Julianne | Ortman | Hennepin County (MN) Sheriff's Office |

Appendixes

| Title | First | Last | Agency/organization |
|---|---|---|---|
| Ms. | Erin | Sindberg Porter | Greene Espel P.L.L.P. |
| Chief | Jeff | Potts | Bloomington (MN) Police Department |
| Assistant Director | Ronald | Ruecker | FBI Office of Law Enforcement Coordination |
| Chief | Raymond | Schultz | Albuquerque Police Department |
| Superintendent | Wade | Setter | Bureau of Criminal Apprehension (MN) |
| Assistant City Manager | Ed | Shikada | City of San Jose, CA |
| Chief | Floyd | Simpson | Corpus Christi Police Department |
| Chief | Tom | Smith | St. Paul Police Department |
| Sheriff | Rich | Stanek | Hennepin County (MN) Sheriff's Office |
| Special Agent in Charge | Lou | Stephens | U.S. Secret Service |
| Chief | Jeff | Tate | Shakopee (MN) Police Department |
| Chief | Scott | Thomson | Camden (NJ) Police Department |
| Deputy Director of Technical Assistance | Jessica | Toliver | Police Executive Research Forum (PERF) |
| Special Agent in Charge | J. Chris | Warrener | FBI-Minneapolis |
| Staff Inspector | Scott | Weidmark | Toronto Police Service |
| Professor | Charles | Wellford | University of Maryland |
| Executive Director | Chuck | Wexler | Police Executive Research Forum (PERF) |
| Chief | Noble | Wray | Madison (WI) Police Department |
| Special Agent in Charge | Bernard | Zapor | Department of Justice-ATF (MN) |